Fishing Virginia

Help Us Keep This Guide Up to Date

Every effort has been made by the authors and editors to make this guide as accurate and useful as possible. However, many things can change after a guide is published—trails are rerouted, regulations change, techniques evolve, facilities come under new management, etc.

We would love to hear from you concerning your experiences with this guide and how you feel it could be improved and kept up to date. While we may not be able to respond to all comments and suggestions, we'll take them to heart, and we'll also make certain to share them with the authors. Please send your comments and suggestions to the following address:

The Globe Pequot Press
Reader Response/Editorial Department
P.O. Box 480
Guilford, CT 06437

Or you may e-mail us at:

editorial@GlobePequot.com

Thanks for your input, and happy trails!

Fishing
Virginia

MARTIN FREED
AND RUTA VASKYS

THE LYONS PRESS
GUILFORD, CONNECTICUT
AN IMPRINT OF THE GLOBE PEQUOT PRESS

The Lyons Press is an imprint of The Globe Pequot Press.

10 9 8 7 6 5 4 3 2 1

Printed in the United States of America

Text design by Casey Shain
Maps created by Tim Kissel/Trailhead Graphics © Morris Book Publishing, LLC
Photos by Martin Freed and Ruta Vaskys

ISBN 978-1-59921-139-8
Library of Congress Cataloging-in-Publication Data is on file.

To all people who enjoy the great outdoors, especially those who actively work to preserve this great resource for future generations. We would like to thank the agencies as well as all the dedicated employees of the Virginia Department of Game and Inland Fisheries, the Virginia Marine Resource Commission, and the USDA Forest Service who are constantly working to improve our sport and the environment. Some of the information in this book is in the public venue and available from the above agencies.

Contents

Dedication v
Introduction. 1
   Overview. 1
   Hazards and Precautions. 1
   Catch-and-release Fishing. 6
   How to Use This Guide 6
   Map Legend 8

Saltwater Fishing

The Eastern Shore. 9
   Angling the Eastern Shore. 9
   Directions to the Eastern Shore 11
The Atlantic Ocean Side 13
   1.   Chincoteague 13
   2.   Assateague Island. 16
   3.   Gargatha 18
   4.   Wachapreague. 19
   5.   Quinby 19
   6.   Oyster 23
The Chesapeake Bay Side. 25
   7.   Saxis. 25
   8.   Onancock Creek 26
   9.   Occohannock Creek 27
   10. Cape Charles 28
   11. Kiptopeke State Park. 30
The Western Shore 32
   12. Colonial Beach. 32
   13. The Great Wicomico River (Reedville Area) 32
   14. Rappahannock River. 35
   15. The Piankatank River 35
   16. Gloucester Point Fishing Pier. 37
   17. Plum Tree Island National Wildlife Refuge 40
   18. James River Bridge. 40
   19. Ocean View Pier 43
   20. Virginia Beach 44
   21. First Landing State Park 46
   22. False Cape State Park 46

Overview

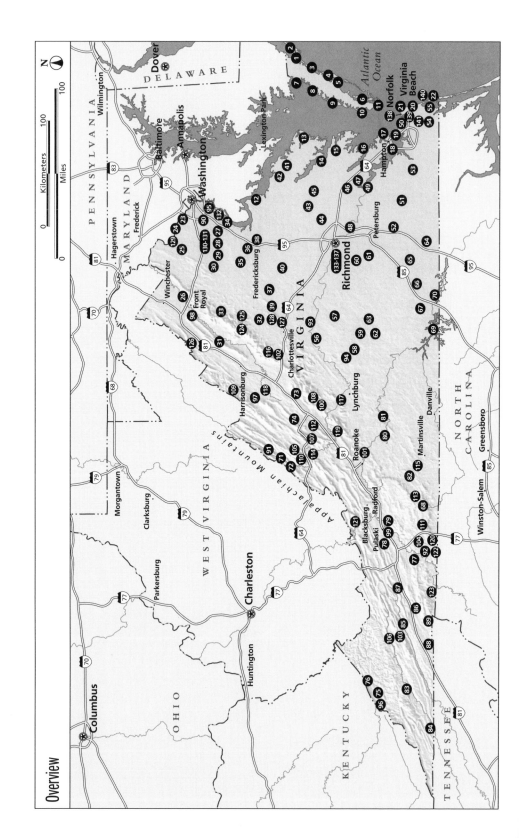

Freshwater Fishing

Northern Virginia..51
23. Great Falls National Park...51
24. Riverbend Park 52
25. Beaverdam Creek Reservoir...53
26. Lake Frederick 54
27. Burke Lake..54
28. The Occoquan River...56
29. Occoquan Reservoir...57
30. Lake Brittle...58
31. The North Fork of the Shenandoah River 59
32. The South Fork of the Shenandoah River..........................62
33. Arrowhead Lake 64
34. Leesylvania State Park..64
35. The Upper Rappahannock River 66
36. Abel Reservoir (Safford County Reservoir)........................68
37. Lake Orange...68
38. The Lower Rappahannock River....................................69
39. Lake Gordonsville (Bowlers Mill)...................................70
40. Lake Anna 71
41. Gardy's Mill Pond 74
42. Chandler's Mill Pond..75
43. The Mattaponi River 75
44. The Pamunkey River...78
45. The Piankatank River/Dragon Run.................................79

Southeastern Virginia 81
46. Diascund Creek Reservoir 81
47. Little Creek Reservoir..83
48. The Lower James River...84
49. The Lower Chickahominy River and Lake 87
50. Lakes Whitehurst and Smith.......................................89
51. Lake Airfield 89
52. The Nottoway River 90
53. Western Branch Reservoir..92
54. The North Landing River...93
55. Back Bay..95

South-central Virginia...97
56. The Upper James River...97
57. Bear Creek Lake...99
58. Holliday Lake 99
59. The Appomattox River...101
60. Pocahontas State Park: Swift Creek Lake and Beaver Lake...........102
61. Lake Chesdin 103
62. Briery Creek Lake...104
63. Sandy River Reservoir..105

64. The Meherrin River 106
65. Brunswick County Lake 107
66. Great Creek Watershed Lake 108
67. Lake Gordon 109
68. The Dan River 109
69. Buggs Island Lake (Kerr Reservoir) 112
70. Lake Gaston 113
Southwestern Virginia 115
71. The Jackson River 115
72. Lake Moomaw 117
73. St. Marys River 118
74. The Maury River 119
75. The Pound River 121
76. Flannagan Reservoir 122
77. The New River 123
78. Gatewood Reservoir 126
79. Claytor Lake 127
80. Smith Mountain Lake 128
81. Leesville Lake 131
82. Philpott Reservoir 131
83. Bark Camp Lake 132
84. The Clinch River 133
85. The North Fork of the Holston River 135
86. The South Fork of the Holston River 136
87. The Middle Fork of the Holston River 137
88. South Holston Reservoir 138
89. The Whitetop Laurel Creek 139
Trout Fishing 141
The Catchable-trout Stocking Program 141
Delayed Harvest Trout Streams 148
90. Accotink Creek (Fairfax County) 148
91. Back Creek (Bath County) 148
92. Chestnut Creek (Carroll County) 148
93. Hardware River (Fluvanna County) 148
94. Holliday Creek (Appomattox/Buckingham Counties) 148
95. Holmes Run (Fairfax County) 149
96. North Fork of Pound River and Pound River (Wise County) 149
97. North River (Augusta County) 149
98. Passage Creek (Warren County) 149
99. Peak Creek (Pulaski County) 149
100. Pedlar River (Amherst County) 149
101. Roanoke River (Roanoke County and City of Salem) 149
102. South River (Augusta County) 149
Fee Trout-fishing Areas 149
103. Clinch Mountain Fee Fishing Area 150

104. Crooked Creek Fee Fishing Area 150
105. Douthat Lake Fee Fishing Area 150
The Fingerling Stocking Program 150
106. Laurel Bed Lake (Russell County) 151
107. Lexington City Reservoir (Rockbridge County) 151
108. Mills Creek and Coles Run Reservoirs (Augusta County) 151
109. Skidmore Lake (Switzer Dam, Rockingham County) 152
110. Smith Creek (Alleghany County) 152
111. Snake Creek (Carroll County) 152
112. Buffalo Creek (Rockbridge County) 152
113. The Dan River (Patrick County) 152
114. Roaring Run (Botetourt County) 152
115. Smith River (Henry County) 153
The Wild Trout Program 153
116. North Fork Moormans River (Albemarle County) 153
117. Buffalo River (Amherst County) 154
118. Ramsey's Draft (Augusta County) 154
119. North Creek (Botetourt County) 154
120. North and South Forks of Stewart's Creek (Carroll County) 154
121. Little Stony Creek (Giles County) 154
122. East Fork of Chestnut Creek (Carroll County) 154
123. Big and Little Wilson Creeks and Their Tributaries (Grayson County) . . 155
124. Conway River/Devils Ditch (Greene County) 155
125. Rapidan River (Madison County) 155
126. Little Stony Creek (Shenandoah County) 155
Trout Heritage Day Program 155

Urban Fishing

Charlottesville 156
127. Ragged Mountain Reservoirs 156
128. Rivanna Reservoir 156
D.C. Metropolitan Area in Virginia 156
129. Algonkian Regional Park 156
130. Cameron Run Regional Park (Lake Cook) 156
131. Fountainhead Regional Park 158
132. Mason Neck State Park 158
Richmond 158
133. Bryan Park 158
134. Byrd Park 158
135. Dorey Park Lake 158
136. Great Shiplock Park 158
137. James River Park 160
Virginia Beach and Surrounding Areas (Hampton Roads) 160
138. Bayville Farms Park 160
139. Lake Prince 160

140. Little Island Park 160
141. Mount Trashmore Lake. 160

Index 161
About the Authors 164

Introduction

Overview

Virginia is a land of contrast. Some say that the Old Dominion is like a miniature United States. This state stretches from the Atlantic Ocean and shining white beaches of the Eastern Shore through the plains of the piedmont to the mountains of the west.

Like the United States, the fishing is as diverse as the terrain. From 600-pound giant tuna in its offshore waters to that evolutionarily aberrant but delicious flounder in the Chesapeake, to oversized bucket mouths in the piedmont lakes to 8-inch brook trout in the bubbling mountain streams, what more can a dedicated angler ask for?

In this book we just give a sampling of what an angler can expect from Virginia. Though over one hundred locations are described, that is just a small number of the total. If you had a few lifetimes, the Old Dominion has more fishing opportunities than anyone could possible expect to try. But we can give it a go.

We wrote this book after a lifetime of fishing and hope the purchaser will enjoy as many hours as we have in pursuit of this sport.

Hazards and Precautions

Snakes

Though the overwhelming majority of snakes in Virginia are harmless and a vital part of the environment, three or four species of the poisonous reptiles are present. While snakebites are rare, anyone venturing into the wilderness should take certain precautions.

Not all snakebites can be prevented, but a few simple steps will greatly reduce the risk:

- Know how to identify poisonous and nonvenomous species.
- Take a snakebite kit and become familiar with its use.
- Know where to go for help.
- Know the most common symptoms of snakebite:
    a) bloody discharge at wound site
    b) fang marks
    c) swelling at the site of the bite
    d) severe localized pain and discoloration
    e) swollen lymph nodes near bite
    f) diarrhea, burning, convulsions, fainting, and/or dizziness

The symptoms may resemble other medical conditions. Consult a physician if you think you've been bitten.

Treatment for snakebites: Stay calm and act quickly. Get help fast but while waiting for assistance, do the following:

1. Wash the bite with soap and water.
2. Keep bitten area lower than the heart.
3. Apply a cool compress.
4. Monitor breathing and heart rate.
5. Remove all rings, watches, and constrictive clothing, in case of swelling.

If unable to get help within thirty minutes, the American Red Cross recommends the following:

- Apply a bandage, wrapped 2 to 4 inches above the bite, to help slow the venom. This should not cut off the flow of blood from a vein or artery—the band should be loose enough to slip a finger under it.
- A suction device can be placed over the bite to help draw venom out of the wound without making cuts. These devices are often included in commercial snakebite kits.

Prevention: The best precaution is to prevent a snakebite to begin with:

- Do not harass any snake or any other wildlife for that matter. Many bites occur as a result of someone trying to kill a snake or get too close to it.
- Do not walk through tall grass unless absolutely necessary. Stick to the hiking paths as much as possible.
- Watch where you put your hands and feet.
- Be especially cautious when rock climbing.

Most important, do not let a fear of snakes stop you from having a good time in the outdoors. Bites are very rare. Just take some precautions.

Insects and Arachnids

These critters are more annoying and some say as dangerous as snakes. However, just a few simple precautions can save the day.

Mosquitoes: These are the most common pest. In some areas of the state, especially the lowlands, they could carry diseases, some that are life threatening. However, they are easily deterred:

- Use a repellent. Many think that the most effective are products that contain deet. The higher the percentage of this ingredient, the better. If you do not want to use deet, Natrapel does work but perhaps not as well.
- Mosquitoes are most active around dusk. Staying indoors during this time will limit exposure.
- Wear clothes covering most of your skin.
- Some people also wear head nets.

No-see-ums or gnats: If you ever had to spend a night dealing with these guys, it will be long remembered. Some call them sand fleas, as they are usually found in sandy or gravelly areas. They are small enough to pass through all but the finest screens. Make sure your tent or camper is so outfitted.

Deet works well and we have spread it on our screens with some success. Since these insects are attracted to light, it is best to do your reading before dark.

Ticks: Various species of ticks are found throughout Virginia. A tick bite from an infected individual can result in a serious disease. Here are a few precautions:

- These guys hang on foliage waiting for a host to walk by. Stay on rocky or sandy trails.
- Rub insect repellent on your legs.
- Wear your pants inside your socks and put repellent on them. White socks are best because the ticks will be easier to spot.
- Check your skin for ticks every evening, or have your partner do it for you.
- If you happen to get a tick bite, keep in mind that the longer the critter is attached, the more likely it is to pass a disease on to you. If you can not get to medical help quickly, take a good pair of tweezers, grab your skin below the tick's mouth, and pull it off. Dab with alcohol and bandage.

Spiders: A few poisonous spiders inhabit Virginia. Very few spider bites are reported. Folks usually get stung when they roll over onto the critter or try to scratch as it is walking up their body. Stay aware of what is going on around you.

Bears

The black-bear population is increasing in the Old Dominion. These guys are very shy and you should consider yourself lucky if you see one. However, a few precautions should be taken not so much to protect humans from bears but the other way around. It's usually the carelessness of humans that produces a nuisance animal, and occasionally one has to be dispatched.

- Always keep your food in bear-proof containers.
- Keep your campsite clean and neat.
- Do not throw garbage out into open receptacles. We've noticed that some areas in the western part of the state now have bear-proof garbage cans.
- Head in the opposite direction, very slowly, if a cub is seen.

Other Mammals

While raccoons, possums, foxes, coyotes, and other mammals are not usually any threat, rabies has been found in Virginia. This disease could make even the shyest critters aggressive. If you see any animal acting strangely, do not approach. Move away.

Poison Ivy and Poison Oak

These plants are common in Virginia. Most people are at least somewhat allergic to the oils produced on their leaves. The best way to protect your yourself is to learn to identify them and make sure you are not exposed. Standard clothing does not help very much. The oil can penetrate the fabric and reach your skin. In fact, you

Be careful of poison ivy. It could spoil a great trip.

can develop the symptoms by touching the clothes after they are taken off. The oils can also be spread person to person. If one is exposed, touching someone else can give them the allergy.

In order not to ruin a trip, take an antihistamine salve along just in case someone develops the rash. A number of good ones can be bought over the counter at most pharmacies. If the condition is severe, seek medical help.

The Sun

The sun is very strong in Virginia during the summer. If you are fair skinned, be sure to include a good sunscreen in your supplies. It should have an SPF value of at least 25.

The best way to treat sunburn is to avoid it. However, if it happens, a number of over-the-counter remedies are available at your pharmacy. These will treat the discomfort and minimize the chances of infection. Mild cases of sunburn can be treated by taking a cool shower or applying cold cloth compresses. The application of topical agents such as aloe vera and/or salves containing hydrocortisone could be helpful.

Severe sunburn and sun poisoning should be treated by a medical professional. Do not wait until you get home—seek medical help at once. Find a local doctor or even an emergency room if necessary to get treatment. The symptoms of sun poisoning are fever, nausea, vomiting, fatigue, dizziness, red skin rash, or chills.

Boating

Be aware of the boating regulations and what equipment is needed. Each vessel should be equipped with one personal floatation device (PFD) for each individual onboard. Make sure that you have the appropriate sizes for kids and adults. Some boats require fire extinguishers, whistles, flares, and running lights. These things do get checked. See the Virginia Department of Game and Inland Fisheries (VDGIF) Web site for specific information (www.dgif.virginia.gov/boating/).

Know Your Limits

Some of the locations, especially those for wild trout, require rigorous hiking. Some of this may be downhill. That means it could be easy heading in, but you will have a more strenuous hike back up. Do not wear yourself out beyond your ability to get back to the parking lot.

Fish Consumption Advisories and Restrictions

The overwhelming majority of fish caught in Virginia are fine for human consumption. However, the Department of Environmental Quality (DEQ) periodically tests fish for contaminants. Currently, most Virginia waters do not have dangerous levels of contaminants, but on occasion some species from certain waters are found to contain chemicals at levels of concern.

For current information on this topic, go to www.vdh.virginia.gov/epi/publichealthtoxicology/fishingadvisories.asp, or call the DEQ at (804) 698-4113.

Hydrilla Weed and Zebra Mussels

These two imported, exotic organisms are very destructive to aquatic ecosystems and have done great damage to lakes and rivers where they have been accidentally introduced. They reduce fish spawning habitat and host a number of parasites that are harmful to fish. The following the steps are recommended to prevent introduction of these pests to uncontaminated waters:
- Do not transfer bait from one body of water to another.
- Do not leave your boat's engine in the horizontal position when in storage. This does not allow all the water to drain out of it.
- Completely drain all water from the trailer.
- Allow the boat and trailer to dry for at least two days before launching into an uncontaminated body of water.
- Inspect the hull and engine for signs of zebra mussels and grass.

If you suspect that you've boated in contaminated waters, wash your boat and trailer with 140 degree F water.

Catch-and-release Fishing

If anglers adhere to the regulations, the fisheries certainly can sustain the harvest. However, over the years catch-and-release has become more popular. In fact, in some delicate Virginia waters, it is required.

Here are a few tips for successfully releasing fish:

- One of the best things an angler can do to reduce harm to fish is to use barbless hooks. These cause a lot less damage to the fish's mouth.
- Make sure you hold the fish gently. Do not squeeze the gut area and never put your hands in the gills. Do not even press on the gill area from the outside.
- Always wet your hand before handling the fish. This helps maintain the slime on the critter's body, which is required for their good health.
- Hold the fish in the stream with its head facing upstream. This will allow a flow of water over its gills and replenish the oxygen lost during the fight. Hold it there until the fish swims away on its own. You can move it back and forth to force water over its gills.
- Many use hooks slightly larger than necessary for the size fish for which they are angling. This reduces the number of deeply hooked fish that are caught. Most will just have the hook in their lips. Needle-nose pliers will always come in handy for unhooking.

Follow these guidelines and most released fish will whip their tails, disappear, and live to fight another day.

How to Use This Guide

This guidebook is arranged into six regional chapters, a separate chapter on trout fishing, and an appendix that covers urban fishing. The first chapter describes salt-water fishing on the Eastern Shore of Virginia. The next chapter describes the angling opportunities along the Western Shore. The Eastern Shore chapter is divided into two parts: the Atlantic Ocean side and the Chesapeake Bay side.

For the purposes of this book, the Western Shore is defined as the saltwater fishing locations within the following boundaries from south to north: east and north of the southern tip of False Cape State Park, following Route 60 north and west to Ocean View. From here a line is drawn to Route 17 in Portsmouth and then the Western Shore follows Route 17 to Route 3. It then follows Route 3 to Kilmarnock and turns north onto Route 200, then west onto Route 360 at Burgess. At Callao it follows Route 202 north and then back to Route 3 to north on Route 305 back to Route 3 to Route 301 to the Potomac River Bridge. If a freshwater lake is within this area, it is included in the adjacent chapter.

The next four chapters comprise the fresh- and brackish-water areas and are divided up as follows: Northern Virginia, Southeastern Virginia, South-central Virginia, and Southwestern Virginia.

The Trout Fishing chapter covers trout fishing in Virginia. It is divided into five parts: Catchable-trout stocking waters, delayed harvest streams, fee fishing areas, fingerling stocking waters, and Wild Trout Program waters. The "catchable" section is divided into counties, then sites are listed by stream or lake name. Directions are given to most. The wild-trout streams are described in the other section. Access points are given for most. In any of these sections, if a body of water was described in detail in another chapter, we refer the reader to that area.

The Appendix describes fishing in urban areas. If the body of water has been described in another chapter, it is noted and the reader is directed to those pages. If not, directions and species available for each body of water are discussed.

For rural areas, where possible, a few campgrounds, lodges, and B&Bs are listed if they're reasonably close to the location.

Directions are given from a nearby town, crossroad, or major highway. The maps are intended to serve as references that will help readers find bodies of water and access points. However, the maps are not intended for navigation. In some cases it was not practical to show all the roads leading to certain access points. We recommend purchasing a detailed road atlas such as the *Virginia Atlas and Gazetteer,* published by DeLorme, to supplement the maps and written directions in this book.

The waters in each chapter are generally listed north to south. If a few are clustered together, we describe them together regardless of their latitude. Rivers do run north–south, so we just estimate their mean latitudinal positions.

If the reader wishes to fish in a certain area, it is best to look at the overview map to obtain the numbers of nearby sites. Then go to the table of contents to find the name of the sites and the page numbers. Specific site maps accompany some of the individual site descriptions throughout the text when the overview map does not provide enough detail.

We do not get too involved with regulations as they periodically change. In some cases but definitely not all, we point out some special regulations that should be checked before fishing. It is up to the reader to keep up to date with the current regulations.

Map Legend

Interstate Highway

U.S. Highway

State Highway

County or Local Highway

Fishing Site

Boat Ramp

Point of Interest

Longitude and Latitude Coordinates

Anglers Reef + 37°44'00" 75°53'00"

Lighthouse

Marina

Park

Wildlife Refuge

Historical Park

Campground

Lake/Reservoir

River

Swamp/Marsh

The Eastern Shore

The Eastern Shore of Virginia has some of the best saltwater fishing available anywhere along the east coast of the United States. Because of the area's unique geographical and demographic characteristics, angling opportunities abound.

The Virginia part of the Eastern Shore is a narrow peninsula with the Atlantic Ocean on one side and the Chesapeake Bay on the other. In some places it is less than 10 miles wide. Because of this, anglers can choose where to fish depending on what they wish to catch and where the run is the strongest at any particular time. It is also convenient when the wind velocities are high. If they are out of the easterly quarter, the bay side is calmer than the seaside. When the winds are westerly, the opposite is true. So fishers have the option of also being in the lee of the wind.

Though changing, the Eastern Shore is still quite rural. As such, there's less fishing pressure than in more populated areas. This makes for more satisfying experiences. Boat ramps are abundant and some shore fishing is available. While a few of the ramps are private—some of which charge a fee—most were built and maintained by the state. Many of these ramps have piers and docks associated with them. At times there is excellent shore-based fishing from these structures.

Angling the Eastern Shore

Saltwater fishing on the Eastern Shore is a year-round activity. Starting in the spring, some years as early as March, the seaside has the earliest run of summer flounder anywhere on the eastern seaboard. Anglers travel from as far as Boston in the north and Florida in the south to participate in this run.

Many are not aware of the fact that it is actually two species of flounder that frequent this area. The overwhelming majority are summer flounder, but as the weather warms, a few southern flounder show up in the mix. They look very similar physically, and differences between the two varieties would probably not be noticed by the average fisher unless he or she were looking for them.

By the end of March, when the water temperatures reach about 45 to 50 degrees F, tautog become active over local rock piles and wrecks. This species is found on both the seaside and bay side.

By late April the first run of croakers begins to show up on the bay side. These fish do not bite as soon as they show up, but the netters start taking them in the more restrictive bodies of water adjacent to the bay.

Meanwhile on the seaside, flounder anglers begin to take a few gray trout (weakfish) on their flounder baits. This usually occurs in late April and continues through June. Some years there are enough trout that many folks actually target the species. Also mixed in with the flounder and trout are a few small-to-medium bluefish. Occasionally a real tackle buster will be caught.

Most years the best flounder fishing on the seaside occurs between May and June. During this time the spring striped-bass (rockfish) season begins in the Chesapeake Bay. This is mostly a trophy season as many large bruisers are taken.

Black drum, the poor man's small-boat big game, begin to show up in May. They run up the Chesapeake while those bound for Delaware Bay swim along the seaside. These guys can tip the scales anywhere from 10 pounds to some in the 80-to-90-pound range.

Flounder fishing is popular along the Eastern Shore.

In Virginia these runs usually last through the second week of June.

By mid-June the waters off the Eastern Shore begin to settle into the typical summer fishery with a variety of fish. Some flounder will still be available on both sides, as well as croakers, speckled trout, gray trout, and some whiting. As the waters warm, some porgies, triggerfish, pigfish (grunts), pinfish, and a few sheepshead begin to show up in the catch.

Sea bass and some porgies begin to take over the rock piles and wrecks, replacing tautog. These guys are usually available through November. This is primarily a seaside activity. Though plenty are caught in the Chesapeake, most are undersized.

This is also the time that cobia begin their annual run, mostly in the lower bay. These guys could run upward of 80 pounds. Spadefish is another summer species that gets a lot of attention. This fishery is mostly in the bay, but many of the offshore wrecks and buoys on the seaside also are havens for spadies.

Midsummer inshore fishing can be hit-or-miss depending the year. However, persistent anglers can catch a respectable amount of varied species. Offshore, trollers and chunkers will usually do very well with various blue-water fish like tuna, bonito, king mackerel, wahoo, and marlin. Closer to home, some will pull various artificials to catch Spanish mackerel.

Usually beginning in mid-September, the best fishing of the year happens and could last through the end of October or early November. On the seaside all the species mentioned previously become very active as they are preparing for their offshore and southerly migrations.

In October the bay side sees its best run of flounder of the year. These are the largest flatfish caught in the waters off the shore. This run can last through December if it doesn't get too cold.

The tautog also become active in October. On the seaside they are mixed with sea bass and become more and more prominent in the catch as the water cools. They also start stirring in the bay. These guys keep biting through December in the bay and all winter off the seaside.

The striped-bass season starts on the bay side in mid-October. The early fish are usually small, and although many throwbacks will be caught, a few legal specimens will be mixed in. As the season progresses, larger rockfish move down the bay and by late November that fishery is in full swing. The Chesapeake Bay rockfish season ends December 31, but many fish can still be caught thereafter, though they would all have to be carefully returned to the water.

On the seaside the first stripers usually show up in November and the season peaks in December. These guys can actually be caught all winter long. Most are at least legal-size and some run up to 50 pounds.

Saltwater fishing off the Eastern Shore of Virginia is probably the best that can be found anywhere along the coast. A great variety is available with little pressure most of the time.

Directions to the Eastern Shore

If you are coming from the north, take the N.J. Turnpike and cross the Delaware Memorial Bridge. Turn south on Route 13. You can stay on Route 13 or take the toll road (Route 1) to Dover, Delaware. It does take fifteen minutes off the trip and costs a couple of bucks. If you took Route 1, at Dover return to Route 13. Follow 13 to

Virginia's Artificial Reef Program Virginia like many other coastal states has an artificial reef program. The Chesapeake and Atlantic seafloor off the coast of Virginia is relatively featureless. Any added structure is almost always a fish attractant. Not only does this concentrate the fish for anglers but it also provides scarce cover for many species.

Beginning in the 1950s, both private organizations and state agencies have been sinking various materials to improve fish habitat. We refer to many of these sites in the text and maps of this book. For more information about Virginia's Artificial Reef Program go to www.mrc.state.va.us/vsrfdf/reef.shtm.

Salisbury, Maryland, then take the bypass, Route 50, which ends again on Route 13. Continue on 13 past Pocomoke City, Maryland, and cross the border into Virginia.

If you are coming from the Washington, D.C.–Baltimore area, take Route 50 across the Chesapeake Bay Bridge. Take the bypass around Salisbury, which ends at Route 13, and then follow the directions discussed above.

From the south, the Norfolk–Virginia Beach area, cross the Chesapeake Bay Bridge Tunnel, which is Route 13.

All directions on the Eastern Shore will start on Route 13.

Distances from Major Metropolitan Areas

New York City: 260 miles
Philadelphia: 176 miles
Washington, D.C.: 155 miles
Baltimore: 156 miles
Norfolk: 25 miles

The Atlantic Ocean Side

Seaside Eastern Shore Species Throughout the Year

Species	Jan.	Feb.	Mar.	April	May	June	July	Aug.	Sept.	Oct.	Nov.	Dec.
Flounder		•	••	•••	•••	••	•	••	••			
Tautog	•••	•••	•••	••	••	•	•	•	•	••	•••	•••
Croaker					•	••	•••	•••	••	•		
Gray trout				•	•	•	•	••	••	••		
Striped bass	•••	••	•						•	•	••	•••
Bluefish				•	•	••	••	••	••	•••	•	
Spot					•	••	••	••	•••	••		
Sea bass					•	•••	••	••	••	••	•••	•
Tuna						•	•	••	••	•••	••	•
King mackerel					•	••	••	•••	••			
Spanish mackerel				•	•	••	•••	•				
Red drum						•	•	•••	••	•		
Black drum				•	•••	•••	•					
Whiting					•	••	••	••	•••	••		
Speckled trout							•	•	••	•		

• Few fish
•• Good fishing
••• Excellent fishing

Note: Though a species may be present, the season may be closed. Always check regulations.

1 Chincoteague

Key species: Inshore: Flounder, sea trout, striped bass, black and red drum, croaker, spot, blue crabs, bluefish, clams. *Offshore:* Sea bass, tautog, large bluefish, tuna, bonito, wahoo, king mackerel, Spanish mackerel.

Best time to fish: April through October.

Directions: Heading south on Route 13, turn left (east) onto Chincoteague Road (Highway 175), located between New Church and Oak Hall. Follow it for 10.4 miles across the drawbridge into the town of Chincoteague.

Description: The town of Chincoteague is located on Chincoteague Island. While this piece of land is considered a barrier island, it is protected by another barrier, which is a few hundred yards seaward.

Chincoteague is a popular tourist destination and there are many second homes on the island. As such there are numerous facilities, including restaurants, motels, hotels, fishing stations, a cinema, and a couple of campgrounds.

Sites 1, 2, 3, 7, and 8

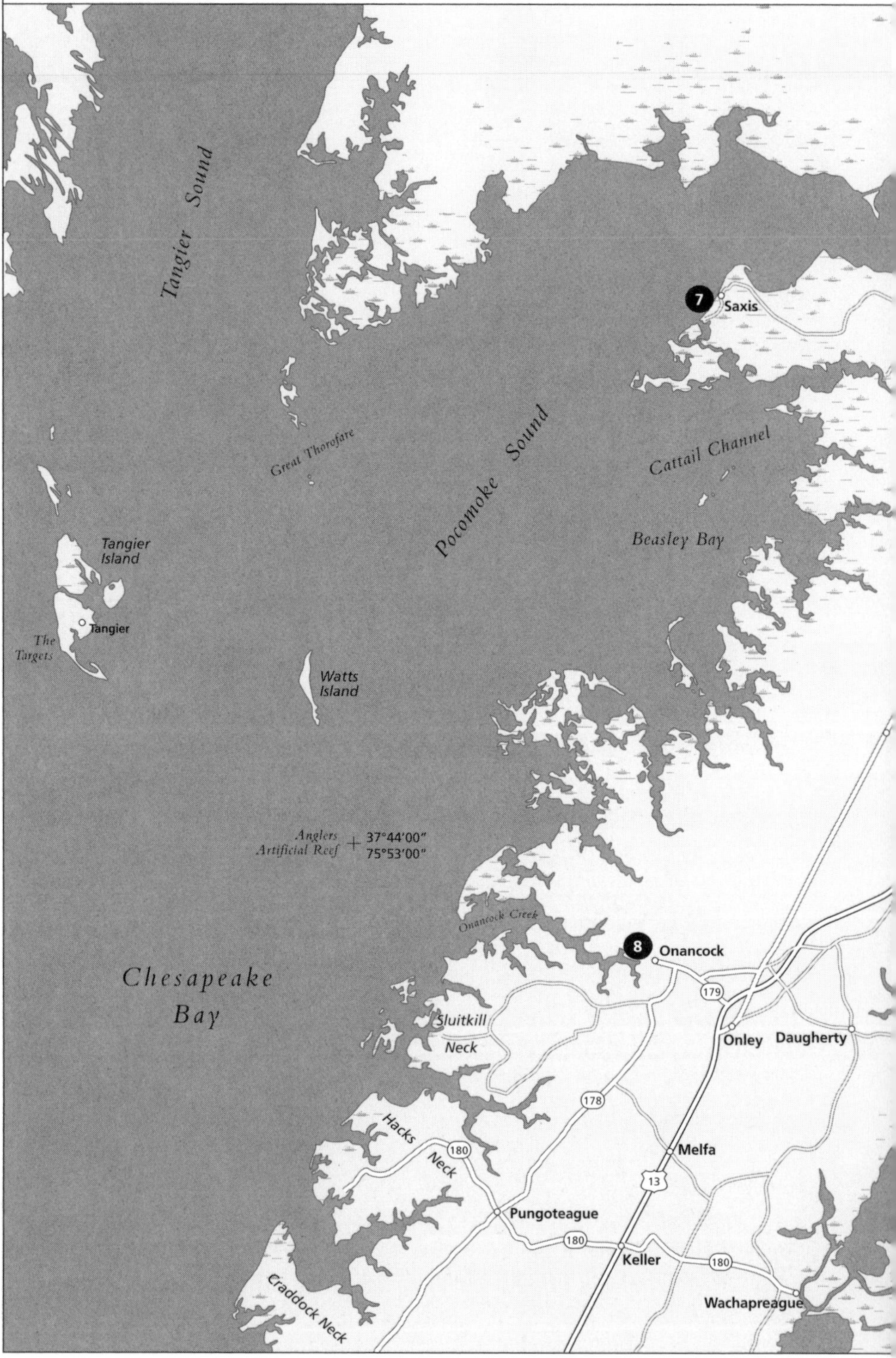

Tangier Sound

7 Saxis

Great Thorofare

Pocomoke Sound

Cattail Channel

Beasley Bay

Tangier
Island

The
Targets

○ Tangier

Watts
Island

Anglers
Artificial Reef + 37°44'00"
75°53'00"

Onancock Creek

8 Onancock

Chesapeake
Bay

179

Sluitkill
Neck

Onley Daugherty

178

Hacks

Melfa

Neck

180

13

Pungoteague

180

Keller

180

Wachapreague

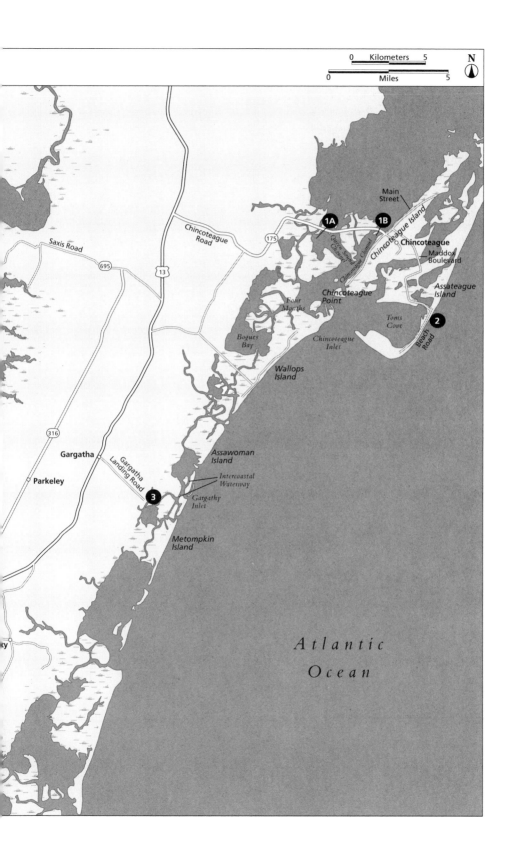

The fishing: Chincoteague is one of the premier early season flounder destinations. One of the best early locations is an area known as Four Mouths. Other earlier season flounder hot spots are the Queen Sound Channel and Chincoteague Point. Early season flatfish anglers usually use live mud minnows dressed up with a strip of squid. Some add bucktail teasers and/or spinners to the hook leaders.

As the season progresses the other species, as described earlier in the "Seaside Eastern Shore Species Throughout the Year" table, begin to show up in the catch. Most fishers switch over to two-hook high-low rigs. The lower hook, size 2 to 6, is tied on a 1-foot leader a couple of inches above the sinker (2 to 6 ounces depending on tide and wind conditions). The second hook, size 1/0 to 3/0 (any style Mustad Ultra-Point is a good choice), is tied on a 2-foot leader 36 to 60 inches above the first. The lower hook is meant for pigfish, spot, croakers, and the like, while the higher one can easily hold trout and blues.

Shore-bound anglers can fish along the seawall at the base on the Chincoteague side of the bridge. In addition, piers may be available at a few of the fishing stations.

Access: There's a Virginia Department of Game and Inland Fisheries (VDGIF) boat ramp on the south side off Highway 175 just before crossing the bridge into the town. There's limited parking at this location (1a). Another ramp (1b) is found in the downtown area. Turn south onto Main Street after crossing the bridge, go 0.5 mile and turn right into parking lot. The ramp is to the west along Chincoteague Channel. Some of the fishing stations also have ramps.

Camping and RV Parks: Maddox Family Campground, 6742 Maddox Blvd., Chincoteague, VA 23336; (757) 336–3111. Pine Grove Campground, 5283 Deep Hole Rd., Chincoteague, VA 23336; (757) 336–5200. Tall Pines Harbor Campground, 8107 Tall Pines Lane, P.O. Box 375, Sanford, VA 23426; (757) 824–0777. Tom's Cove Family Campground, 8128 Beebe Rd., Chincoteague, VA 23336; (757) 336–6498.

For more information: Barnacle Bill's Bait and Tackle, 3691 Main St., Chincoteague Island, VA 23336; (757) 336–5920; www.barnaclebillsbaitandtackle.com/index.html. Sea Hawk Sport Center, 643 Ocean Hwy., Pocomoke City, MD 21851; (410) 957–0198; www.seahawksports.com. Chincoteague Chamber of Commerce, P.O. Box 258, Chincoteague, VA 23336; (757) 336–6161; www.chincoteaguechamber.com. Virginia Marine Resources Commission (VMRC), 2600 Washington Ave., Third Floor, Newport News, VA 23607; (800) 541-4646; www.mrc.state.va.us.

2 Assateague Island (see map on pages 14-15)

Key species: Striped bass, bluefish, flounder, sea trout, red drum, croaker, spot, bluefish, whiting.

Best time to fish: April through January.

Directions: Heading south on Route 13, turn left (east) onto Chincoteague Road (Highway 175), located between New Church and Oak Hall. Follow it for 10.4 miles across the drawbridge. After crossing the bridge onto Chincoteague, make a left (north) onto Main Street. Follow Main a few blocks, then turn right onto Maddox Boulevard. Maddox makes a few turns and goes around a circle eventually becoming Beach Road. Follow this across a bridge to Assateague Island.

Description: Assateague Island is composed of the Chincoteague National Wildlife Refuge and the Assateague National Seashore. An entrance fee applies but as with many national wildlife refuges, if you have a Federal Migratory Bird Stamp, access is free.

Assateague Island is the site of many wildlife and birding festivals. A big event that draws many visitors is the annual pony roundup. These diminutive horses probably originally arrived on the island as a result of a shipwreck in the eighteenth or nineteenth century. They've done so well that a number of them have to be taken off the refuge every year or they would interfere with native wildlife. As a result, many are rounded up and sold at auction to help fund the local fire department.

The fishing: Assateague Island is one of the few ocean beach areas on the Eastern Shore that can be reached by foot or vehicle. The others require a boat to access. The island is about 37 miles long, a large portion of that in Maryland. Every inch of the beach has fish-holding potential.

The fishing actually never ends. Striped bass are often present all winter long. In April other species begin to show up. One favorite is whiting, which makes fine table fare. Though small (maximum 3 pounds or so), these guys are quite scrappy. Bluefish also begin to show up at this time. Though most will be a pound or two, occasionally a real slammer picks up the bait of some unsuspecting surf caster. (Surf casting is the best way to fish this area.) The other fish species that also may be taken between April and November are spot, croaker, red drum, both species of trout, and flounder.

The beach stretches for many miles to the south and also into Maryland to the north. Vehicle traffic is restricted, so check at the office or booth on current regulations.

Camping: Though Maryland allows camping on their part of the island, none is permitted in Virginia. However, a few campgrounds are available in Chincoteague. Many restaurants, nightclubs, hotels, motels, and other facilities are nearby.

For more information:. Seahawk Sport Center, 643 Ocean Hwy., Pocomoke City, MD 21851; (410) 957–0198; www.seahawksports.com. Chincoteague Chamber of Commerce, www.chincoteaguechamber.com. Lots of information about Assateague, including festivals, hiking trails, and other events and attractions, can be found at www.assateague.com. Virginia Marine Resources Commission (VMRC), 2600 Washington Ave., Third Floor, Newport News, VA 23607; (800) 541-4646; www.mrc.state.va.us.

3 Gargatha *(see map on pages 14-15)*

Key species: Flounder, sea trout, striped bass, black and red drum, croaker, spot, blue crabs, bluefish, clams.

Best time to fish: April through October.

Directions: Heading south on Route 13, pass Nelsonia, turn left (east) onto Gargatha Landing Road (Route 680), and follow it to the end.

Description: Gargatha is very rural. Any services will be found along Route 13.

The fishing: Gargatha is one of the early season flounder destinations. While some locals use it, fishing pressure is light. One of the best early locations is in the Intercoastal Waterway both north and south of the inlet. Try to drift or troll up the slopes of the channel.

For those who enjoy surf casting, on most days, unless it is very rough, you can beach your boat on the sand in the inlet. You can cast right there or walk around the beach to a better-looking location. *PLEASE NOTE:* Some of this is private property. Therefore, stay in the tidal area. Also, during the spring, piping plovers nest in the grass. Please do not disturb them.

Fly-fishers do well in the inlet. Anything that imitates a mullet or menhaden will work. Some deep holes are present right along the shore.

As the season progresses the other species, as shown on the "Seaside Eastern Shore Species Throughout the Year" table, begin to show up in the catch. Most fishers switch over to two-hook high-low rigs. The lower hook, size 2 to 6, is tied on a 1-foot leader a couple of inches above the sinker (2 to 6 ounces depending on tide and wind conditions). The second hook, size 1/0 to 3/0 (Mustad Ultra-Point is a good choice), is tied on a 2-foot leader 36 to 60 inches above the first. The lower hook is meant for pigfish, spot, croaker, and the like, while the higher one can easily hold trout and blues.

Access: There's a Virginia Department of Game and Inland Fisheries (VDGIF) boat ramp at the end of Gargatha Landing Road.

Camping and RV Parks: Maddox Family Campground, 6742 Maddox Blvd., Chincoteague, VA 23336; (757) 336–3111. Pine Grove Campground, 5283 Deep Hole Rd., Chincoteague, VA 23336; (757) 336–5200. Tall Pines Waterfront Campground and RV Park, 8107 Tall Pines Lane, P.O. Box 375, Sanford, VA 23426; (757) 824–0777. Tom's Cove Family Campground, 8128 Beebe Rd., Chincoteague, VA 23336; (757) 336–6498.

For more information: Seahawk Sport Center, 643 Ocean Hwy., Pocomoke City, MD 21851; (410) 957–0198; www.seahawksports.com. Barnacle Bill's Bait and Tackle, 3691 Main St., Chincoteague Island, VA 23336; (757) 336–5920; www.barnaclebillsbait andtackle.com/index.html. Peace Token, (757) 824–5068. Virginia Marine Resources Commission (VMRC), 2600 Washington Ave., Third Floor, Newport News, VA 23607; (800) 541-4646; www.mrc.state.va.us.

4 Wachapreague *(see map on pages 20–21)*

Key species: Inshore: Flounder, sea trout, striped bass, black and red drum, croaker, spot, blue crabs, bluefish, clams. *Offshore:* Sea bass, tautog, large bluefish, tuna, bonito, wahoo, king mackerel, Spanish mackerel.

Best time to fish: April through October.

Directions: Heading south on Route 13, past Melfa and Route 734, turn left (east) onto Wachapreague Road (Route 180) and follow it to the end.

Description: Wachapreague is known as the Little City by the Sea. It is a small community with lots of facilities and is therefore a popular tourist destination. A couple of restaurants, a motel, and a few fishing stations are available for tourists.

Fishing tournaments that take place in the area include Captain Zed's Bait and Tackle Spring Flounder Tournament in April, the Wachapreague Marina Spring Flounder Tournament, also in April, and the Wachapreague Women's Tuna Tournament in summer, usually some time in July.

The fishing: Wachapreague is known among fishers as the flounder capital of the world and therefore one of the premier early season flounder destinations. The flat-fishing usually begins in an area known as Green and Drawing Channel. Early season flatfish anglers usually use live mud minnows dressed up with a strip of squid. Some add bucktail teasers and/or spinners to the hook leaders.

See the table at the beginning of this chapter for more information on the best months for catching various species on the seaside Eastern Shore.

Shore-bound anglers can fish along the docks. This area is very productive late in the season. Many trout and whiting can be taken, especially at night under the lights.

Access: The city has its own boat ramp and a couple of the fishing stations each have one.

Lodging and Camping: Fisherman's Lodge Marina and Campground, Atlantic Ave., Wachapreague, VA 23480; (757) 787-4913. Wachapreague Motel, 17 Atlantic Ave., Wachapreague, VA 23480; (757) 787–2105.

For more information: Captain Zed's Bait and Tackle, 17 Atlantic Ave., Wachapreague, VA 23480; (757) 789–3222. Wachapreague Marina, 15 Atlantic Ave., Wachapreague, VA 23480; (757) 787–4110; www.wachapreaguemarina.com. General tourist information can be found at www.wachapreague.com. Virginia Marine Resources Commission (VMRC), 2600 Washington Ave., Third Floor, Newport News, VA 23607; (800) 541-4646; www.mrc.state.va.us.

5 Quinby *(see map on pages 20–21)*

Key species: Inshore: Flounder, sea trout, striped bass, black and red drum, croaker, spot, blue crabs, bluefish, clams. *Offshore:* Sea bass, tautog, large bluefish, tuna, bonito, wahoo, king mackerel, Spanish mackerel.

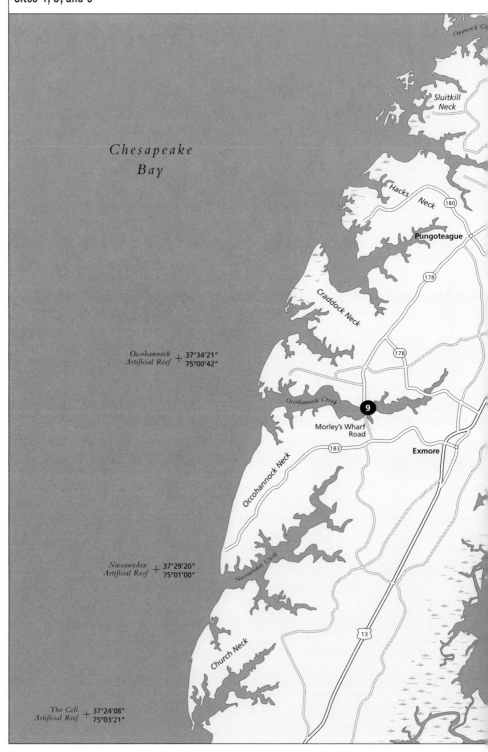

Chesapeake
Bay

Onancock Cr

Sluitkill
Neck

Hacks Neck (180)

Pungoteague

(178)

Craddock Neck

(178)

Occohannock
Artificial Reef + 37°34'21"
75°00'42"

Occohannock Creek

9

Morley's Wharf
Road

(183) Exmore

Occohannock Neck

Nassawadox
Artificial Reef + 37°29'20"
75°01'00"

Nassawadox Creek

(13)

The Cell
Artificial Reef + 37°24'08"
75°03'21"

Church Neck

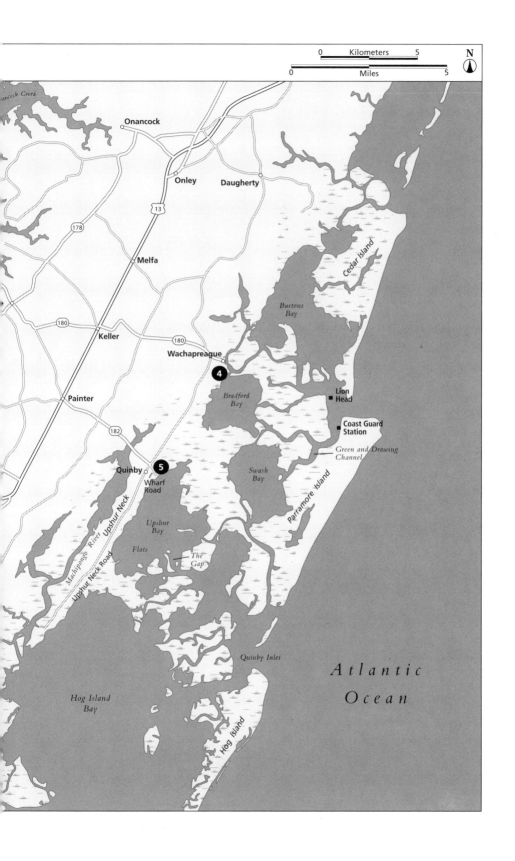

Quinby is a great launch point for Eastern Shore fishing sites.

Best time to fish: April through October.

Directions: Heading south on Route 13, in Painter turn left (east) onto Quinby Bridge Road (Route 182). Follow it across the bridge to the end and make a right (south) onto Upshur Neck Road. Follow Upshur and turn left (east) onto Wharf Road. The dock and ramp are at the end of this road.

Description: Quinby is a small town just a few miles south of Wachapreague. In the past it received very little pressure. This has changed as it has been discovered. There are a couple of B&Bs in Quinby. Restaurants and motels can be found in Wachapreague or along Route 13. Bait is available in Quinby.

The fishing: Quinby is another of the early season flounder locations. Some of the best flatfishing is almost right outside the harbor. Either drift or troll along the channel edges. As the season progresses, the flounder spread out and some are even caught on the flats.

See the table at the beginning of this chapter for more information on the best months for catching various species on the seaside Eastern Shore.

Shore-bound anglers can fish along the docks at the harbor. This is very productive late in the season. Many trout and whiting can be taken, especially at night under the lights. You can also fish alongside the bridge over the Machipongo River, just as you are entering Quinby. *NOTE:* It is illegal to fish from the bridge.

Access: There's a fine two-boat ramp in Quinby with a big parking lot.

Lodging: The Fisherman's Lodge, 20210 Harbor Point Rd., Quinby, VA 23423; (757) 442–7109; www.fishermanslodge.com. Wachapreague Motel, 17 Atlantic Ave., Wachapreague, VA 23480; (757) 787–2105.

For more information: Captain Zed's Bait and Tackle, 17 Atlantic Ave., Wachapreague, VA 23480; (757) 789–3222. Wachapreague Marina, 15 Atlantic Ave., Wachapreague, VA 23480; (757) 787–4110; www.wachapreaguemarina.com. Virginia Marine Resources Commission (VMRC), 2600 Washington Ave., Third Floor, Newport News, VA 23607; (800) 541-4646; www.mrc.state.va.us.

6 Oyster

Key species: Flounder, sea trout, striped bass, black and red drum, croaker, spot, blue crabs, bluefish, clams.

Best time to fish: April through October.

Directions: Heading south on Route 13 turn left (east) onto Townfield Drive (Route 680). Follow this to the town of Cheriton and make a right (south) onto Business Route 13. In 1 block make a left (east) onto Sunnyside Road (Route 639). This road ends in Oyster.

Description: Oyster is a small fishing town. There are a few clam houses, but it is basically a sleepy little village. Restaurants, motels, and the like can be found in Cape Charles or along Route 13.

The fishing: Oyster is another of the early season flounder locations. Being in the far south area of the peninsula, many folks coming from the Hampton Roads (a local name for the cities in southeast Virginia) use it as a jumping-off point.

Oyster is one of first areas where black drum show up in the spring—late April or May. The fish are caught right outside the harbor.

See the table at the beginning of this chapter for more information on the best months for catching various species on the seaside Eastern Shore.

Access: There's a fine two-boat ramp with a big parking lot.

Camping and RV Parks: Cherrystone Family Camping and RV Resort, 1511 Townfields Dr., Cheriton, VA 23316; (757) 331–3063; www.cherrystoneva.com. Kiptopeke State Park, (757) 331–2267; www.dcr.state.va.us/parks/kiptopek.htm.

For more information: Chris' Bait and Tackle, 28316 Lankford Hwy., Capeville, VA 23313; (757) 331–3000; www.chrisbaitandtackle.com. Bailey's Bait and Tackle, 327 Mason Ave., Cape Charles, VA 23310; (757) 331–1982. Virginia Marine Resources Commission (VMRC), 2600 Washington Ave., Third Floor, Newport News, VA 23607; (800) 541-4646; www.mrc.state.va.us.

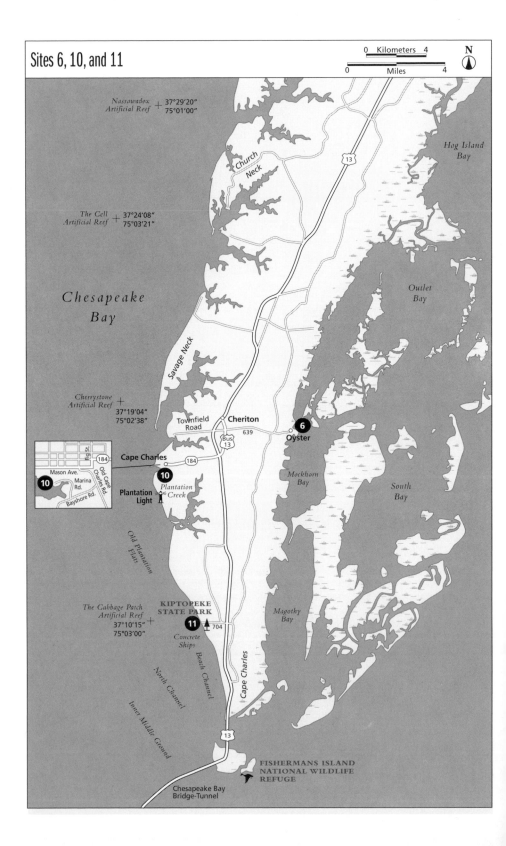

0   Kilometers   4

0   Miles   4

N

Nassawadox Artificial Reef + 37°29'20" 75°01'00"

Church Neck

13

Hog Island Bay

The Cell Artificial Reef + 37°24'08" 75°03'21"

Chesapeake Bay

Outlet Bay

Savage Neck

Cherrystone Artificial Reef + 37°19'04" 75°02'38"

Townfield Road

Cheriton

639

6 Oyster

Bus 13

Cape Charles

184

184

10

Plantation Creek

Mockhorn Bay

South Bay

Fig St.

184

Old Cape Charles Rd.

Mason Ave.

Marina Rd.

10

Bayshore Rd.

Plantation Light

Old Plantation Flats

The Cabbage Patch Artificial Reef 37°10'15" 75°03'00" +

KIPTOPEKE STATE PARK

11 ↟ 704

Magothy Bay

Concrete Ships

North Channel

Beach Channel

Cape Charles

Inner Middle Ground

13

FISHERMANS ISLAND NATIONAL WILDLIFE REFUGE

Chesapeake Bay Bridge-Tunnel

The Chesapeake Bay Side

Chesapeake Bay Side Eastern Shore Species Throughout the Year

Species	Jan.	Feb.	Mar.	April	May	June	July	Aug.	Sept.	Oct.	Nov.	Dec.
Flounder				•	•	•••	••	••	••	•••	•••	••
Tautog	••	•	••	••	••	•			•	••	••	•••
Croaker				•	••	•••	••	••	•••	•		
Gray trout				•	•	•	•	••	••	••		
Striped bass				•	••	•			•	•	••	•••
Bluefish				•	•	••	••	••	••	•••	•	
Spot					•	••	••	••	•••	•		
Cobia					•	•••	•••	•••	••	•		
Red drum					•	•	•	•	•••	••		
Black drum				•	••	•••	•		•	•		
Spanish mackerel					••	•••	••					
Spadefish					•	••	•••	•••	••			
Sheepshead								•	•			
Speckled trout				•	••	•••	••	••	•••	••	•	

• Few fish
•• Good fishing
••• Excellent fishing

7 Saxis (see map on pages 14-15)

Key species: Croaker, gray and speckled trout, striped bass, red drum, spot, flounder, blue crabs.

Best time to fish: May through December.

Directions: Heading south on Route 13, turn right (west) onto Saxis Road (Route 695) in Temperanceville. The boat ramp is at the end of this road.

Description: Saxis is a small, sleepy fishing village a good drive off the main road. It's a nice place to get away from the frenzy, as few drive that far to fish. All services are found on Route 13.

The fishing: Saxis is one of the best areas to launch for fishing in Pocomoke and Tangier Sounds. Because its restricted waters warm quickly, it is one of the earliest areas where croaker and trout are caught each year. The Target Ships at Smith and Tangier Islands are relatively short runs. Sea trout, croaker, spot, red drum, whiting, and striped bass are all possible at the Saxis Fishing Pier (see below). No fee is required, but a Virginia Saltwater License is.

Access: The 200-foot Saxis Fishing Pier, with a 100-foot T at the end, is an excellent place for land-based anglers. It is wheelchair-accessible and lit twenty-four hours a day. There's also an excellent accessible boat ramp.

Camping: Tall Pines Harbor Campground, 8107 Tall Pines Lane, Sanford, VA 23426; (757) 842–0777; www.tallpinesharbor.com.

For more information: The Eastern Shore Chamber of Commerce, (757) 787–2460; www.eschamber.com. Sea Hawk Sport Center, 643 Ocean Hwy., Pocomoke City, MD 21851; (410) 957–0198; www.seahawksports.com. Virginia Marine Resources Commission (VMRC), 2600 Washington Ave., Third Floor, Newport News, VA 23607; (800) 541-4646; www.mrc.state.va.us.

8 Onancock Creek (see map on pages 14-15)

Key species: Croaker, gray and speckled trout, striped bass, red drum, spot, flounder, blue crabs.

Best time to fish: May through December.

Directions: Heading north on Route 13, in Onley turn left (west) onto Route 179 (Onancock Road) and follow it through the town to the harbor. The ramp is located next to the harbor master's office.

Description: Onancock is an artsy community with antiques shops, galleries, an assortment of restaurants, a movie theater, a playhouse, and a good hardware store. A few B&Bs are in town, while motels are located in nearby Onley.

The fishing: The fishing here is about the same as that at Occohannock Creek. Plenty of opportunities exist in the creek on the way out to the bay. Open bay fishing is also excellent out of this port. It is also a great launching point for excursions to Watts and

Black drums like this one are Chesapeake Bay's big game.

Tangier Islands. Big gray trout are caught on the Chesapeake side of Tangier at a place known as the Targets. They were used in the past as targets for fighter jets.

The area known as Onancock–Pungoteague Flats is quite famous for producing speckled trout, bluefish, striped bass, and even cobia. Look for grass beds and cast soft plastic leadhead jigs for specks and rock; troll large spoons for cobia.

Angler's Reef is just a short distance off the mouth of the creek. It is an excellent location to try for large migrating stripers in the fall and assorted bottom fish during the entire season.

Access: There's an excellent boat ramp at the town harbor with a big parking lot.

Camping and RV Parks: Kiptopeke State Park, (757) 331–2760; www.dcr.state.va .us/parks/kiptopek.htm. Cherrystone Family Camping and RV Resort, 1511 Townfields Dr., Cheriton, VA 23316; (757) 331–3063; www.cherrystoneva.com.

For more information: The Eastern Shore Chamber of Commerce, (757) 787–2460; www.eschamber.com. Information about the harbor can be found at www.onancock .com/harbor.htm. Harbor Master: (757) 787–7911.

For fishing information, contact the Wachapreague Marina (757–787–4110) or Captain Zed's Bait and Tackle, 17 Atlantic Ave., Wachapreague, VA 23480; (757) 789–3222. Virginia Marine Resources Commission (VMRC), 2600 Washington Ave., Third Floor, Newport News, VA 23607; (800) 541-4646; www.mrc.state.va.us.

9 Occohannock Creek *(see map on pages 20–21)*

Key species: Croaker, gray and speckled trout, striped bass, red drum, spot, flounder, blue crabs, bluefish, spadefish.

Best time to fish: May through December.

Directions: Heading north on Route 13, in Exmore turn left (west) onto Occohannock Neck Road (Route 183), at a traffic light. Follow that about 4 or 5 miles to Morley's Wharf Road (Route 608) and make a right (north). At the end of this lane is the dock and ramp.

Description: The ramp and pier at Morley's Wharf is in a very rural area. All services can be found along Route 13. An excellent country store run by the Rampasaud family is in the nearby town of Belle Haven.

The fishing: Occohannock Creek is just one of the many creeks and rivers that branch off from the Chesapeake Bay and wind into the Eastern Shore. These areas are natural fish hatcheries and not only attract some spawning fish species but also predators that hunt many smaller varieties.

The creek has a maximum depth of over 40 feet. Fishing can be good in any amount of water depending on the species sought and the time of year. Many anglers will fish right at the mouth where the creek enters the Chesapeake, but good angling can actually be found almost anywhere.

This is also a great location to test your skills at angling for the elusive speckled trout. Some fly-fish for this species. These guys are primarily shallow fish and it is best to locate grass beds. Many cast soft plastic leadhead jigs for specks. Bait like soft crabs also works but because there are so many "pickers," this can be an expensive proposition. If you are after these guys or stripers, fish the edges of the shore, bars, and channels.

Occohannock Artificial Reef is just a short boat ride out of the creek. Be sure to follow markers as there are many shallow bars in the area. The reef is an excellent location for large migrating rockfish as well as many bottom-dwelling species.

Shore-bound anglers will find a really nice pier at the ramp at Morley's Wharf. Many fine fish are taken from this structure, but it is particularly good for striped bass late in the season: November and December. Many cast soft plastics under the lights during an outgoing tide.

Access: There's an excellent and free boat ramp at Morley's Wharf with a big parking lot.

Camping and RV Parks: Kiptopeke State Park, (757) 331–2760; www.dcr.state.va .us/parks/kiptopek.htm. Cherrystone Family Camping and RV Resort, 1511 Townfields Dr., Cheriton, VA 23316; (757) 331–3063; www.cherrystoneva.com.

For more information: Northampton County Chamber of Commerce, (757) 331–2304; www.northamptoncountychamber.com. The Eastern Shore Chamber of Commerce, (757) 787–2460; www.eschamber.com. Virginia Marine Resources Commission (VMRC), 2600 Washington Ave., Third Floor, Newport News, VA 23607; (800) 541-4646; www.mrc.state.va.us.

For more fishing information, contact Chris' Bait and Tackle, 28316 Lankford Hwy., Capeville, VA 23313; (757) 331–3000; www.chrisbaitandtackle.com; or Bailey's Bait and Tackle, 327 Mason Ave., Cape Charles, VA 23310; (757) 331–1982.

10 Cape Charles (see map on page 24)

Key species: Flounder, sea trout, striped bass, black and red drum, croaker, spot, blue crabs, bluefish, tautog, spadefish.

Best time to fish: April through December.

Directions: From Route 13 about 10 miles north of the Chesapeake Bay Bridge-Tunnel, at the traffic light, make a left (west) onto Stone Road (Route 184). In about a mile make a left (south) onto Fig Street, then a right (west) onto Mason Avenue. In 1 block make a sharp left (south) onto Old Cape Charles Road (Route 642), over the bridge to a right (south) onto Bayshore Road. Proceed 1 block, make another right (west) onto Marina Road, and follow it to the end, where the boat ramp is located.

To get to the beach, continue straight on Mason Avenue instead of turning onto Route 642. The public beach is at the end of the road. The new pier is located here.

Description: The city of Cape Charles has made a real resurgence in the past few years. It was very run-down, with closed businesses and decaying buildings. Now the downtown area is the location of a couple of art galleries, antiques and gift shops, a pharmacy, an art center and theater, and restaurants.

The fishing: Many of the same areas accessible from Kiptopeke State Park are also reachable from Cape Charles. However, it is a longer boat ride in most cases. Keep in mind that there is a substantial charge for the ramp at Kiptopeke and none at Cape Charles. So depending on how much fuel your boat uses, it may be less expensive to launch at Cape Charles.

Spade fish like this beauty are summer visitors to Chesapeake Bay.

In addition to locations described in the Kiptopeke section below (the Concrete Ships, the Chesapeake Bay Bridge-Tunnel, the Cabbage Patch and Plantation Flats), the mussel beds off buoy no. 10 and the rocks at Plantation Light, which are very close to the harbor entrance, are excellent locations for many species, including 'tog, croaker, trout, whiting, red and black drum, and flounder.

The areas called The Cell and the Cherrystone Artificial Reef are also within range of those who launch out of Cape Charles. The former is well known for spadefish, which can be available from June through September, while the latter holds tautog, stripers, and other predators.

Surf casters and jetty jockeys can pursue their sports at the beach in the park at the end of Mason Street. A nice pier has recently opened here.

Access: There's an excellent boat ramp at Cape Charles, next to a big parking lot.

Camping and RV Parks: Kiptopeke State Park, (757) 331–2760; www.dcr.state.va.us/parks/kiptopek.htm. Cherrystone Family Campground and RV Park, 1511 Townfields Dr., Cheriton, VA 23316; (757) 331–3063; www.cherrystoneva.com.

For more information: Go to the Northampton County Chamber of Commerce Web site (www.northamptoncountychamber.com) or call (757) 331–2304. Virginia Marine Resources Commission (VMRC), 2600 Washington Ave., Third Floor, Newport News, VA 23607; (800) 541-4646; www.mrc.state.va.us.

For more fishing information, contact Chris' Bait and Tackle, 28316 Lankford Hwy., Capeville, VA 23313; (757) 331–3000; www.chrisbaitandtackle.com; or Bailey's Bait and Tackle, 327 Mason Ave., Cape Charles, VA 23310; (757) 331–1982.

Successful or not, fishers enjoy the pier at Kiptopeke State Park. Note the concrete ships in the background.

11 Kiptopeke State Park *(see map on page 24)*

Key species: Flounder, sea trout, striped bass, black and red drum, croaker, spot, blue crabs, bluefish, tautog, spadefish.

Best time to fish: April through December.

Directions: From Route 13 south, make a right (west) onto Route 704 about 2 miles before the toll booths at the Chesapeake Bay Bridge-Tunnel. Drive to the entrance booth and pay appropriate fees. Follow directions to ramp and pier.

Description: Kiptopeke State Park has just about every amenity that one can expect at the best state parks. They even have cabins and RVs to rent. An entry fee and charges for most extras apply.

The fishing: Kiptopeke is a jumping off point for many great fishing locations. A short distance from the boat ramp, the concrete ships loom gray and eerie. These were World War II vessels constructed of concrete to avoid detection by radar. After the conflict they were sunk and now they are fantastic fish attractors. Species such as gray trout, tautog, striped bass and many others may be found around the ships depending on the time of year.

A few miles to the south the Chesapeake's largest fish magnet can be found: The Chesapeake Bay Bridge-Tunnel. This 17-mile-long structure is a favorite with many anglers. Tautog fishing around the man-made stone islands and over the tubes of the tunnel is excellent. Rockfish can also be found all around the islands as well as the pilings that hold up the edifice. Other species include bluefish, black and red drum, large trout, spadefish, and sheepshead.

The Cabbage Patch, a few miles off the park is a favorite of black drum anglers and Plantation Flats is the site of cobia and red drum action. Many speckled trout fishers find Plantation Creek a hotspot.

A fine fishing pier at Kiptopeke provides lots of action as does the beach for surf casters. The south beach is particularly productive.

Access: An excellent pay-for two-boat ramp at Kiptopeke with a big parking lot.

Camping and RV Park: Kiptopeke State Park, (757) 331–2760; www.dcr.state.va.us/parks/kiptopek.htm.

For more information: Kiptopeke State Park, 3540 Kiptopeke Dr., Cape Charles, VA 23310; (757) 331–2267; www.dcr.state.va.us/parks/kiptopek.htm. Virginia Marine Resources Commission (VMRC), 2600 Washington Ave., Third Floor, Newport News, VA 23607; (800) 541-4646; www.mrc.state.va.us.

For more fishing information, contact Chris' Bait and Tackle, 28316 Lankford Hwy., Capeville, VA 23313; (757) 331–3000; www.chrisbaitandtackle.com; or Bailey's Bait and Tackle, 327 Mason Ave., Cape Charles, VA 23310; (757) 331–1982.

The Western Shore

The Western Shore is privileged to have an abundance of facilities for sports fishers. This also means that they do get more crowded at times. We only list a few of the many areas that may be of interest.

12 Colonial Beach

Key species: While all Chesapeake species are caught here, croaker and stripers are the most popular.

Best time to fish: April through November.

Directions: From Fredericksburg, take Route 3 east to 205 east to 205Y east.

Description: Colonial Beach is a beach resort town with numerous facilities, places to stay, and second homes. It is located on the lower Potomac River.

The fishing: Croaker are the big attraction here, but striped bass and sea trout are also caught. Some fish for flounder by drifting along the beaches and channel edges. Most of the extensive beach is available for surf casting. The best baits to use are bloodworms, squid, and cut fish, and jigs and swimming lures for stripers.

During autumn, anglers will find excellent rockfishing out of Colonial Beach. Some years bluefish make a good showing.

Access: Route 205Y takes you to the waterfront. Turn south on Monroe Bay Avenue and follow it to the ramp. There's a public pier near the end of 205Y.

Camping: Monroe Bay Campground, Route 658, Colonial Beach, VA 22443; (804) 224–7418.

For more information: Potomac River Charters, (804) 224–1400; www.potomac rivercharters.com. Colonial Beach Chamber of Commerce; www.colonial beach.org. Virginia Marine Resources Commission (VMRC), 2600 Washington Ave., Third Floor, Newport News, VA 23607; (800) 541-4646; www.mrc.state.va.us. Potomac River Fisheries Commission, 222 Taylor St., P.O. Box 9, Colonial Beach, VA 22443; (804) 224–7148 or (800) 266–3904; www.prfc.state.va.us.

13 The Great Wicomico River (Reedville Area)

Key species: Striped bass, croaker, spot, bluefish, specks and gray trout, flounder, crabs. At times white perch are abundant.

Best time to fish: May through December.

Site 13

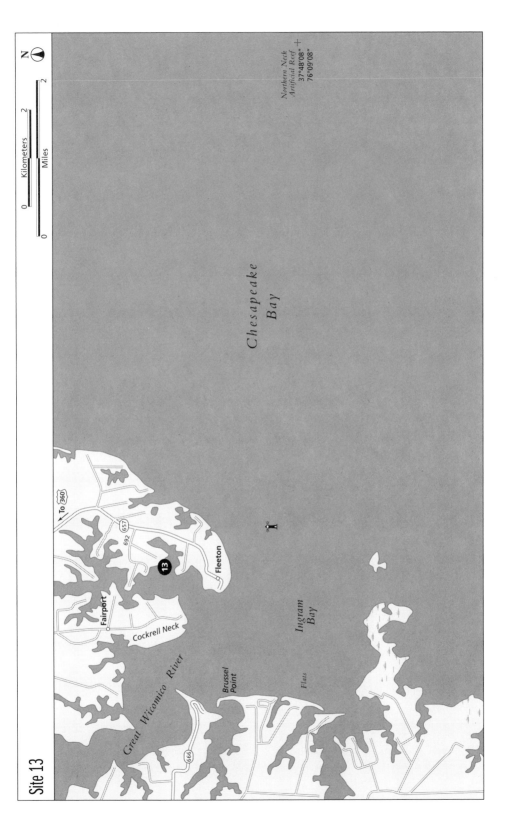

Chesapeake
Bay

Northern Neck
Artificial Reef
37°48'08"
76°09'08"

To 360

692 657

13

Fairport

Cockrell Neck

Fleeton

Great Wicomico River

Brussel
Point

666

Ingram
Bay

Flats

N

Kilometers
0   2

Miles
0   2

Fishers enjoy a beautiful summer day on the pier at Colonial Beach.

Directions: From Kilmarnock, take Route 200 north to Burgess. Turn east onto 360, then right (south) onto 657 and right (west) on 692, Shell Landing Road, to the ramp.

Description: Reedville is a large town with most amenities. It is a popular destination among anglers. The Great Wicomico River is a estuary that runs into the Chesapeake near the mouth of the Potomac. A number of salty species run up the river to spawn.

The fishing: The access ramp is relatively close to good fishing holes like the mouth of the Potomac. Shore fishing is possible. This is a good launching point to get to the Targets off Tangier and Smith Islands. The Northern Neck Artificial Reef is nearby. The marsh areas around Ingram Bay are also excellent for speckled and gray trout. The best baits to use here are sea worms, jigs, minnows, and squid.

Access: The ramp here is good, and plenty of parking is available.

For more information: Virginia Marine Resources Commission (VMRC), 2600 Washington Ave., Third Floor, Newport News, VA 23607; (800) 541–4646; www .mrc.state.va.us.

14 Rappahannock River (Saltwater) *(see map on page 36)*

Key species: Striped bass, croaker, spot, bluefish, specks and gray trout, flounder, blue crabs.

Best time to fish: April through December.

Directions: From Kilmarnock, take Route 3 south. Cross the Rappahannock River Bridge. Continue south on Route 3. Turn east onto Route 621 and follow it to Locklies Marina.

Description: The Rappahannock is another large river that runs into the Chesapeake Bay from the Western Shore. Most of the Chesapeake's species make feeding and/or spawning migrations up this river. This provides anglers with lots of opportunities to encounter their quarry.

The fishing: This area gives access to the mouth of the Rappahannock River as well as the Chesapeake Bay. Fishing areas like Parrott Island and Windmill and Stingray Points are nearby. The Gwynns Island Artificial Reef is not too long a boat ride from here. Some head across the bay to the Cell, another artificial reef. The marshy areas around Mosquito Island provide some speckled trout action. The best baits to use in this area are squid, sea worms, and various saltwater lures.

Access: The directions provided above are to Locklies Marina, which has a private ramp. Others are also nearby.

For more information: Locklies Marina, P.O. Box 517, Topping, VA 23169; (804) 757–2871 or (888) 860–1040; www.lockliesmarina.com. Virginia Marine Resources Commission (VMRC), 2600 Washington Ave., Third Floor, Newport News, VA 23607; (800) 541-4646; www.mrc.state.va.us.

15 Piankatank River (Saltwater) *(see map on page 36)*

Key species: Croaker, spot, striped bass, speckled trout.

Best time to fish: May through October.

Directions: From Harmony Village, follow Route 3 south toward the Piankatank River Bridge. The ramp is located on the northeast side of the bridge. Make a left-hand (east) turn about ¼ mile before the bridge, then a quick right (south) onto a gravel road, which runs down to the river alongside the bridge.

Description: This backwater of the Chesapeake Bay is very picturesque and productive.

The fishing: There's good croaker fishing in the spring and summer. Striped bass and trout are also quite common. The former are usually here in good numbers during the fall. Try fishing the bay for trout. The best baits to use in this area are sea worms, bucktail and plastic leadhead jigs, and swimming lures.

Sites 14 and 15

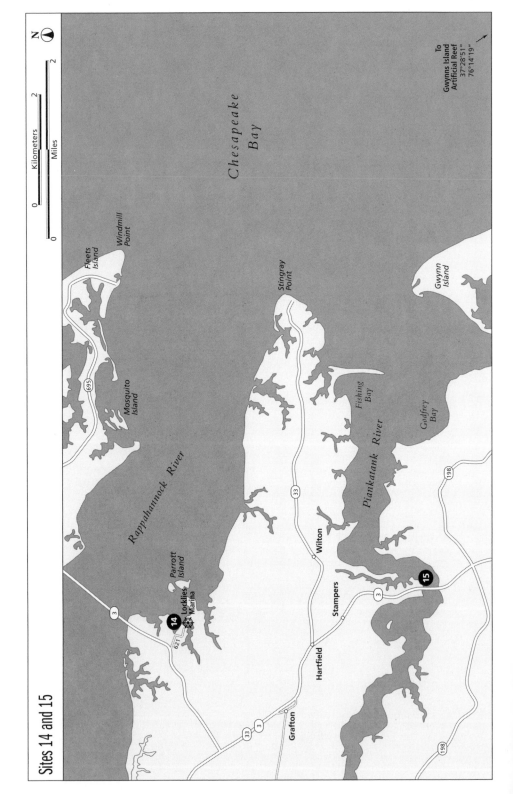

N

Kilometers
0   2

Miles
0   2

Rappahannock River

Fleets
Island

Windmill
Point

Mosquito
Island

695

*Chesapeake
Bay*

Stingray
Point

Parrott
Island

Locklies
Marina

14

621

3

Wilton

33

Piankatank River

Fishing
Bay

Godfrey
Bay

Gwynn
Island

Stampers

3

Hartfield

15

198

Grafton

33
3

198

To
Gwynns Island
Artificial Reef
37°28'51"
76°14'19"

The pier at Gloucester Point is a fine place to fish.

Access: There's a fair, gravel ramp, which is not suitable for big boats. Very limited parking.

For more information: Virginia Marine Resources Commission (VMRC), 2600 Washington Ave., Third Floor, Newport News, VA 23607; (800) 541-4646; www.mrc.state.va.us.

16 Gloucester Point Fishing Pier

Key species: Croaker, spot, Chesapeake Bay's other species.

Best time to fish: May through December.

Directions: From Yorktown, head north on Route 17 across the Coleman Memorial Bridge, which crosses the York River. Make the first right (east), then another right (south), and follow that back and under the bridge.

Description: The pier has a T at the end and is run by the county parks department. A few benches are provided for the comfort of anglers and plenty of parking is available right next to the structure. The Virginia Marine Institute is located within walking distance and they occasionally offer tours. These events are of interest to fishers.

Sites 16 and 17

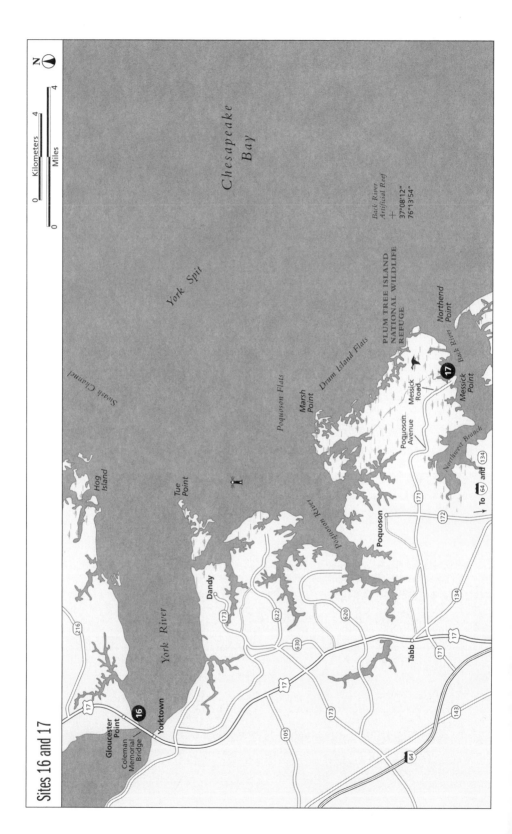

The fishing: Besides croaker and spot, this pier provides nice catches of striped bass, flounder, and gray trout. The best baits for this area are squid and bloodworms.

The Back River Artificial Reef is a short distance to the southeast from the mouth of the York River. The marshes around Tue Point and Hog Island are usually good for specks and other game fish during the summer and autumn. Try fishing around dusk.

Access: There's a good boat ramp here, plus a big parking lot.

For more information: Gloucester County Parks, Recreation and Tourism Dept., P.O. Box 157, Gloucester, VA 23061; (804) 693–2355; www.gloucesterva.info/. Virginia Marine Resources Commission (VMRC), 2600 Washington Ave., Third Floor, Newport News, VA 23607; (800) 541-4646; www.mrc.state.va.us.

Kayak fishing is popular at the Plum Tree Island NWR.

17 Plum Tree Island National Wildlife Refuge (see map on page 38)

Key species: Flounder, speckled trout, croaker, spot, striped bass, blue crabs.

Best time to fish: April through December.

Directions: From Interstate 64, go east on Route 171 (Little Florida Road), which turns into Poquoson Avenue. Take this east. After it curves south, go east on Messick Road and continue to the end. Pay close attention to these directions as it could be confusing for those not familiar with the area.

Description: Located in Poquoson, this wildlife refuge has a fine boat ramp with an ample parking lot. It is located on the relatively protected waters of Back River, yet the Chesapeake is very close.

The fishing: All the Chesapeake Bay species may be caught out of this port. Flounder fishing is particularly good in the Back River and the nearby Chesapeake Bay. Bank fishing is possible. Minnows, squid, and sea worms are the best baits to use here.

This is a good launch point to get to Gwynns Island Artificial Reef, and Back Island Artificial Reef is also within reach. All the marsh areas around Plum Tree Island are excellent for specks.

This is also a favorite launch point for kayakers and fly-fishers.

For more information: Plum Tree Island National Wildlife Refuge, Outdoor Recreation Planner, Charles City Sub-office, 11116 Kimages Rd., Charles City, VA 23030-2844; (804) 829–9020; www.fws.gov/refuges/profiles/index.cfm?id=51512. Virginia Marine Resources Commission (VMRC), 2600 Washington Ave., Third Floor, Newport News, VA 23607; (800) 541-4646; www.mrc.state.va.us.

18 James River Bridge

Key species: Croaker, spot, trout, striped bass.

Best time to fish: April through mid-December.

Directions: The pier is in Newport News, located at the base of the northwest corner of the Route 17 James River Bridge. Traveling north on Route 17, cross the James River Bridge. You will see the pier off to the left as you approach the northern end of the bridge. Make the first left after the bridge into Huntington Park. Lots of parking is available at the base of the pier.

Description: This pier was the old James River Bridge. When the new structure was built, it was left in place and converted into a fishing pier. Being about ½ mile in length, it is known as one of the longest fishing piers on the East Coast. It's a great place for a family outing, and cleaning tables with running water are provided.

The fishing: Croaker fishing is the feature here. When the fish are running, the pier

Casting off the shore at Ragged Island WMA can be effective. The James River Bridge is in the background.

becomes quite crowded, especially on holiday weekends. April appears to be best for the hardheads. As the season progresses, gray trout become common. Many folks will fish at night for weakfish. Striped bass, including some very large individuals, are also caught here. The best baits to use here are squid, bloodworms, clams, and cut bait.

The marshy areas across the river at the Ragged Island WMA are good for many game fish. This is a good launch point for the Hampton Roads Bridge-Tunnel, which is a striper hot spot.

The Ragged Island WMA is located on the south side of the James River Bridge. It is on the east side of the road. Bank casters can do well here with the same species that are caught off the pier. Parking is ample but a short walk is required.

Both the Middle Ground and East Ocean View Artificial Reefs are nearby.

Access: A boat ramp with ample parking is located right next to the pier in Huntington Park. There's also a small beach for surf casting.

For more information: James River Bridge Fishing Pier, 6701 River Rd., Newport News, VA 23602; (757) 247–0364. Virginia Marine Resources Commission (VMRC), 2600 Washington Ave., Third Floor, Newport News, VA 23607; (800) 541-4646; www.mrc.state.va.us.

Sites 18 and 19

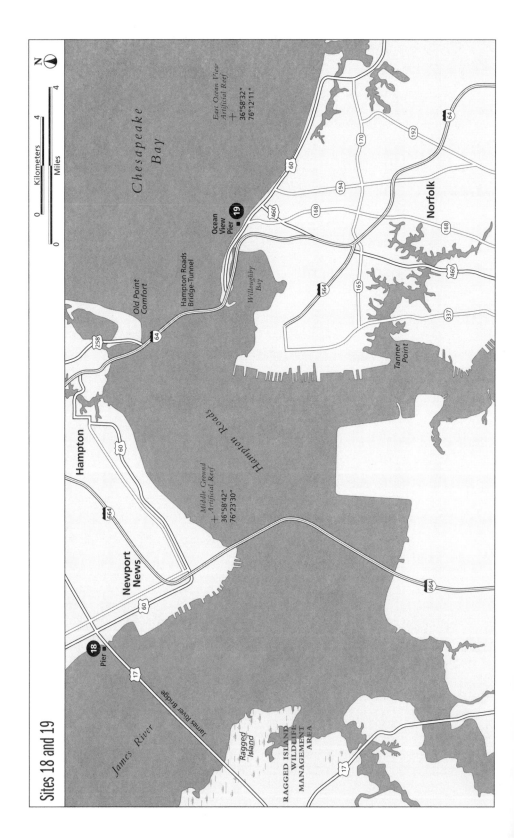

N

Kilometers
0   4

Miles
0   4

Chesapeake Bay

East Ocean View
Artificial Reef
+
36°58'32"
76°12'11"

Ocean View
Pier ■ **19**

Old Point
Comfort

Hampton Roads
Bridge-Tunnel

Willoughby
Bay

Norfolk

Tanner
Point

Hampton

Hampton Roads

Middle Ground
+ Artificial Reef
36°58'42"
76°23'30"

Newport
News

James River

James River bridge

Pier ■ **18**

RAGGED ISLAND
WILDLIFE
MANAGEMENT
AREA

Ragged
Island

19 Ocean View Pier *(see map on page 42)*

Key species: Croaker, flounder, cobia, red drum, striped bass, crabs, spot.

Best time to fish: April through November.

Directions: From Interstate 64 in Norfolk, take Route194 (Chesapeake Boulevard) north to Route 60 northwest to the pier.

Description: This is a modern facility with a long pier with a T at the end. There's also a full-service tackle-and-bait shop, a grill, and a really nice deck overlooking the pier. Cleaning tables with running water are provided.

The fishing: Though most come here to fish for croaker and spot, many large species are also taken. Along with some nice flounder, an occasional cobia and even red and black drum are caught. In fact, some years see an excellent run of the "red ones." The best baits to use here are squid, sea worms, and cut fish.

This happy fisher caught this croaker off the Ocean View Pier.

For more information: Ocean View Fishing Pier, 400 W. Ocean View Ave., Norfolk, VA 23503; (757) 583–6000; www.oceanviewfishingpier.com. Virginia Marine Resources Commission (VMRC), 2600 Washington Ave., Third Floor, Newport News, VA 23607; (800) 541-4646; www.mrc.state.va.us.

20 Virginia Beach

Key species: All the species described in the seaside and bayside "Species Throughout the Year" tables in the Eastern Shore chapters.

Best time to fish: April through December.

Directions: Virginia Beach is accessible from the north and west by Interstate 64 from Richmond. (Near Richmond this road crosses Interstate 95, which is the primary north/south road along the East Coast.) Take I-64 to Interstate 264 and follow this to the end and the beach.

Description: Virginia Beach is large city with an extensive beach. Much of this is open for surf casting. All facilities are available.

The fishing: Just about every type of saltwater fishing is available from Virginia Beach. From giant tuna and marlin offshore to spot and croaker off docks and piers. We will list a very few of the facilities available to fishers. Most saltwater baits will work depending on species sought. Some of the favorites are squid, sea worms, clams, and cut bait.

This is a good location to get to some of the offshore areas like the Chesapeake Bay Tower and Triangle reef. The Chesapeake Bay Bridge-Tunnel is very close.

Access: The Lynnhaven Boat Ramp is located off Route 60 under the Lesner Bridge (757) 460–7590.

To reach Rudee Inlet in Owls Creek from Virginia Beach, proceed south on General Booth Boulevard.

Lynnhaven Pier, 2350 Starfish Rd., Virginia Beach; (757) 481–7071.

Little Island Pier, 3820 S. Sandpiper Rd., Virginia Beach; (757) 426–7200.

Virginia Beach Fishing Pier, 1506 Atlantic Ave., Virginia Beach; (757) 428–2333.

Sea Gull Fishing Pier, Chesapeake Bay Bridge-Tunnel, P.O. Box 5588, Virginia Beach; (757) 464–4641.

Camping and lodging: Besides First Landing State Park, a number of campgrounds are located in Virginia Beach. Here are just a few: Virginia Beach Campground KOA, 1240 General Booth Blvd.; (757) 428-1444. Holiday Trav-L-Park, 1075 General Booth Blvd.; (757) 425-0249. North Landing Beach Campground, 161 Princess Anne Road; (757) 426-6241.

Outside of Virginia Beach camp at Sandy Point Resort Campgrounds, 176 Sandy Point Dr., Knotts Island, NC 27950; (252) 429-3094; or Chesapeake Campground, 693 George Washington Hwy. S., Chesapeake, VA; (757) 485-0149.

Of course, Virginia Beach is large resort town full of hotels, motels, and other

Sites 20, 21, 138, 140, and 141

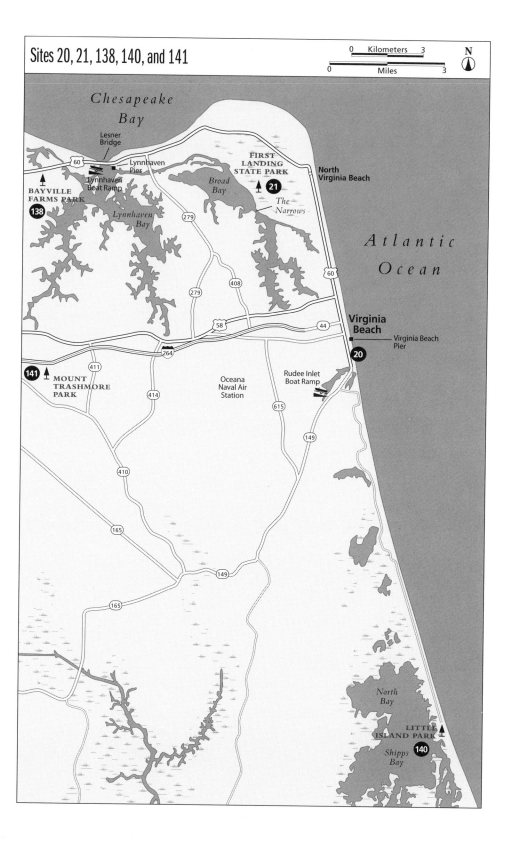

Chesapeake Bay

Lesner Bridge

60

Lynnhaven Pier

Lynnhaven Boat Ramp

BAYVILLE FARMS PARK

138

Lynnhaven Bay

Broad Bay

FIRST LANDING STATE PARK

21

The Narrows

North Virginia Beach

279

408

279

58

264

411

414

410

165

165

149

149

141

MOUNT TRASHMORE PARK

Oceana Naval Air Station

615

Rudee Inlet Boat Ramp

44

Virginia Beach

20

Virginia Beach Pier

Atlantic Ocean

149

North Bay

LITTLE ISLAND PARK

140

Shipps Bay

places to stay. Here are just a few: Econo Lodge on the Ocean, 2707 Atlantic Ave.; (757) 428-3970. Colonial Inn, 2809 Atlantic Ave.; (757) 428-5370. Holiday Inn Sunspree on the Ocean, 3900 Atlantic Ave., (888) 400-9714.

For more information: Long Bay Pointe Bait and Tackle, 2109 W. Great Neck Rd., Virginia Beach, VA 23451; (757) 481–7517 (Captain Steve); www.longbaypointebait andtackle.com. Virginia Beach Fishing Station, 200 Winston Salem Ave., Virginia Beach, VA 23451; (757) 491–8000 or (800) 725–0509; www.virginiafishing.com. Virginia Marine Resources Commission (VMRC), 2600 Washington Ave., Third Floor, Newport News, VA 23607; (800) 541-4646; www.mrc.state.va.us.

21 First Landing State Park *(see map on page 45)*

Key species: All the species described in the "Chesapeake Bay Side Eastern Shore Species Throughout the Year" table in The Chesapeake Bay Side chapter, plus crabs along the docks.

Best time to fish: April through November.

Directions: From Interstate 64, take Route 13 north to 60 east. Follow it to the park entrance.

Description: The park has the attraction of three indoor aquariums. As Virginia's most popular state park, more than a million people visit it every year.

The fishing: The park has a 1½-mile-long beach for surf casting. Many fish and crabs can be found at the Narrows. The best baits to use here are squid, sea worms, clams, and cut bait.

Camping and cabins: Both are available at the park.

For more information: First Landing State Park, 2500 Shore Dr., Virginia Beach, VA 23451-1415; (757) 412–2300; www.state.va.us/dcr/parks/1stland.htm. Virginia Marine Resources Commission (VMRC), 2600 Washington Ave., Third Floor, Newport News, VA 23607; (800) 541-4646; www.mrc.state.va.us.

22 False Cape State Park

Key species: Salt water: Striped bass, whiting, spot, sharks, skates, bluefish. *Freshwater:* Largemouth bass, crappie, white perch, channel catfish.

Best time to fish: May through November.

Directions: This area can not be reached with personal land vehicles. Visitors have to hike or bike in or come by boat. The state park service does have a vehicle called the *Terra Gator,* which is designed to minimize impact on the environment. For a fee, visitors may ride this bus. But only those who hike or bike are allowed to camp.
Reservations are required to ride the *Terra Gator.* It departs Virginia Beach

Folks bundle up for some 'tog fishing off the Sea Gull Pier on the Chesapeake Bay Bridge-Tunnel.

from Little Island City Park at 3820 Sandpiper Road at 9 A.M. and returns at 1 P.M. In the winter it operates only on weekends. Call 1-800-933-7275 (PARK) to make reservations or e-mail falsecape@dcr.virginia.gov. When the *Gator* reaches False Cape, visitors have two hours to fish or explore trails and the natural beach.

Hikers and bikers must park at Little Island City Park, and a fee applies. If you are going to camp overnight, a confirmation letter from the park must be displayed on the front dashboard. Otherwise, your car will be towed. Access to the park is by boat or a beach trail through Back Bay Wildlife Refuge.

To canoe into the park, launch from Little Island Park. Docks are provided for larger craft at Barbour Hill and False Cape Landing, near the Back Bay sites.

Description: The park is just south of Back Bay National Wildlife Refuge. It is a mile-wide barrier spit between Back Bay and the Atlantic Ocean. The park features one of the last undisturbed coastal environments on the East Coast.

The fishing: All the saltwater species that run along the coast can be caught at False Cape. While fishing is good from May through November, the best surf casting is

Saltwater Fishing: The Western Shore

47

in the autumn. The best baits for saltwater fishing are bloodworms, cut bait, clams, and shrimp. The best fishing method here is surf casting.

Camping: Primitive camping is allowed but only to those who hike or bicycle through the wildlife refuge.

For more information: False Cape State Park, 4001 Sandpiper Rd., Virginia Beach, VA 23456; (757) 426–7128; www.state.va.us/dcr/parks/falscape.htm. Virginia Marine Resources Commission (VMRC), 2600 Washington Ave., Third Floor, Newport News, VA 23607; (800) 541-4646; www.mrc.state.va.us. Back Bay National Wildlife Refuge, www.fws.gov/backbay/.

Giant Sea Bass: A Great Winter Diversion

I was being chased by a giant ugly fish. In my panic something kept scratching the back of my brain: I had never seen this species before. Though my boat was heading away from the critter at 30 knots, it was overtaking us. Just a few feet from the stern, it opened its mouth and I saw the massive curved and corkscrew teeth dripping with a combination of seaweed, saliva, and blood. It was just about to swallow us whole, when from deep inside the throat of this genetic aberration came an awful and horrible scream.

Awakening with a start, I realized that the scream was the captain blowing the horn of the *Jil Carrie,* indicating that it was time to unzip the sleeping bag, stand up, and start fishing.

The trip actually began many hours earlier. I left the Eastern Shore at 11:00 P.M. and got to Virginia Beach at 12:30 A.M.. Captain Jim on the *Jil Carrie* was due to sail at 2:00 A.M. so I stood around the deck talking with a bunch of the boys that had gotten there even earlier. One fellow remarked that he arrived at 6:00 P.M. "I just cannot sleep the night before going out on trip like this. Too excited."

The conversation was a combination of self-horn-blowing and complaining. Sometimes in the same breath, these guys would brag about some great catch and then talk about some awful captain they sailed with years ago. In other words they were saying: "If I catch fish, it's because I'm a great fisherman. If I don't catch fish, it's because of the lousy captain." No personal responsibility these days but all part of the game.

When the boat finally left the dock, after listening to all the hot air, I was ready for a nap. After opening up the sleeping bags and rolling my jacket up for a pillow, I don't think it was more than a few seconds before oblivion. The next thing I heard was the boat's horn.

By the time I got out on the deck, fish were being brought over the rail. And they were large. They looked like 10-pounders but were probably closer to 4 or 5. My rod and reel was loaded with 30-pound test Gamma Copolymer line and a 16-ounce sinker. Three number 5/0 Mustad Ultrapoints were strung from just above the sinker to about 4 feet above the bottom. I loaded a glob of cut sea clams on each hook and swung the rig over the rail.

I was surprised at how long it took to get to the bottom but then I realized how deep the water was about 250 feet. No sooner did the sinker hit the bottom than the telltale tap tap of life down below presented itself. I jerked back on the rod and started reeling, but it soon became evident that there was nothing there but the sinker. No problem: I dropped it back down and within a few seconds had one hooked. The rod almost bent in half and I did not think I was going to get the critter off the bottom. Slowly, the fish gave a little ground—or should I say water—and I was able to make a few turns on the reel. It was not a trivial struggle, and all the way to the top my arms ached. Swinging the 4-pound sea bass over the rail, I was wondering how I was ever going to continue to do this for the rest of the day.

Quickly unhooking the fish and rebaiting, I dropped the line into the water and it headed for the bottom. The line suddenly stopped going out. I knew what this was—something picked up the bait on the way down. After engaging the reel, the rod started bouncing like a basketball in the

The Jil Carrie, *seen here at the Long Point Marina, offers long distance sea bass trips in the winter.*

hands of a skilled dribbler. What a battle and what a mess. By the time the 10-pound bluefish was brought to the boat, it had tangled six lines. Nobody was sure who caught the fish, but I was the only one who wanted it anyway, so it was dropped into my cooler. Guess those guys never had smoked bluefish. The mates did a great job and quickly untangled the bird's nest of lines.

I actually filled my twenty-five sea bass limit by 8:30 A.M. and spent the rest of the day helping others get their fish.

The four-hour boat ride back to the dock was calm, and I slept, so that I'd be alert for the drive back to the Eastern Shore. It was a great trip. Worth all the effort. It was the first time in my life that I could not budge the cooler. Needed four mates to help lift it into the pickup.

This trip is highly recommended. A great boat, great crew, and great fishing grounds.

The *Jil Carrie* runs out of Virginia Beach all winter. Contact Captain Jim at (410) 867–4944 or captjim@erols.com (www.azinet.com/captjim).

Northern Virginia

Northern Virginia is very diverse. From the urban areas around Washington, D.C., to the mountains of the west, the angler has a great variety of fishing choices.

23 Great Falls National Park

Key species: Catfish, bass, American eels. Shad pass through in the spring.

Best time to fish: All year.

Directions: Heading north on the Capital Beltway (Interstate 495), past the junction for Route 267 and Elmwood Estates, take Georgetown Pike (Route 193) west to Route 738 north and proceed to the park.

Fishing off the pier at Chandler Mill Pond can produce bass, crappie, and catfish.

Description: This 800-acre park is part of the George Washington Memorial Parkway. It is located along the Potomac River 14 miles upriver from Washington, D.C. It is a beautiful place situated near the nation's capital.

The fishing: Fishing is permitted anywhere along the banks of the river. The most common fishing spots are in Fisherman's Eddy, between Overlooks 1 and 2, and along the shore above the falls. The best baits are minnows, worms, cut bait, and shad darts.

Special regulations: No wading because of dangerous currents. A Maryland or Virginia license is required of everyone over sixteen years of age. Maryland regulations apply. This is a national park so no digging of worms is allowed.

For more information: Great Falls National Park, 9200 Old Dominion Dr., McLean, VA 22101; (703) 285–2965 or (703)

Fisher showing off a nice winter crappie caught out of the northern Potomac.

285–2966; www.nps.gov/gwmp/grfa/. Maryland Department of Natural Resources, 80 Taylor Ave., Annapolis, MD 21401; toll-free in Maryland (877) 620–8DNR (8367), outside of Maryland (410) 260–8367; www.dnr.state.md.us/sw_index_flash.asp.

24 Riverbend Park

Key species: Smallmouth and rock bass.

Best time to fish: All year.

Directions: Take the Capital Beltway (Interstate 495) to exit 44 and head west on Georgetown Pike (Route 193) to a right (north) on River Bend Road. Then turn right (east) on Jeffery Road to the park entrance.

Description: This pretty park on the Potomac close to the D.C. metro area is part of the Fairfax County Park system.

The fishing: This is a great place to fish from a car-top boat, canoe, or kayak. Small-mouth and rock bass are abundant, as are sunfish. There's no white water in this area of the Potomac.

The best baits to use in this area are night crawlers, minnows, and crawfish.

Special restrictions: Open 7:00 A.M. until dusk. No large boats or jet skis. Beware of the dangerous dam downstream. Maryland or Virginia freshwater licenses required. Also, remember that Maryland controls the fishing in the main stem of the Potomac, so be sure follow that state's regulations, not Virginia's.

Access: The park has a nice boat ramp.

For more information: Riverbend Park Visitors Center, 8700 Potomac Hills St., Great Falls, VA; (703) 759-9018; www.fairfaxcounty.gov/parks/riverbend/river info.htm. Maryland Department of Natural Resources, 80 Taylor Ave., Annapolis, MD 21401; toll-free in Maryland (877) 620–8DNR (8367), outside of Maryland (410) 260–8367; www.dnr.state.md.us/sw_index_flash.asp.

25 Beaverdam Creek Reservoir

Key species: Largemouth bass, crappie, channel catfish, carp, white perch.

Best time to fish: March through November.

Directions: From Leesburg, head south on Evergreen Mills Road. Make a left (east) onto Route 629 (Reservoir Road) and follow it to the lake.

Description: This reservoir is in Loudon County but is run by the City of Fairfax. It is over 350 acres, however, access is limited.

The fishing: Good populations of bass and channel cats are featured in this reservoir. White perch found their way into this lake and are now available in good numbers. Anglers are encouraged to fish for this species because they have a tendency to overpopulate and become stunted.

The best baits to use are plastics, small jigs, and surface lures, plus live minnows and night crawlers, and commercial baits for cats and corn for carp.

Fly patterns: bass bugs and poppers.

Access: Old boat ramps are visible but they have been blocked off due to security concerns. Boat anglers will have to carry their crafts about 100 yards. Parking is limited to about five or six vehicles.

For more information: Virginia Department of Game and Inland Fisheries (VDGIF), 1320 Belman Rd., Fredericksburg, VA 22401; (540) 899–4169; www.dgif .virginia.gov/fishing/.

26 Lake Frederick

Key species: Bass, walleye, sunfish, crappie, northern pike, catfish.

Best time to fish: March through November.

Directions: Take Route 340 north about 5 miles from Front Royal. Look for the public fishing lake sign.

Description: Lake Frederick is an impounded lake, covers over 100 acres, and is owned by the Virginia Department of Game and Inland Fisheries (VDGIF). Many people fish from the bank. Gasoline engines are prohibited, but electric motors are okay. Sunken trees and stumps are used by predators for cover and are good areas to toss a lure.

The fishing: Frederick is known for large redear and bluegill sunfish. The lake supports a good population of bass that keeps the numbers of panfish down thereby allowing the remainder of the sunfish to grow to prodigious sizes.

Excellent largemouth bass are taken from Frederick every year. Some are 10-pounders and many are in the 3-to-8-pound range. They could be difficult to catch due to the lake's very clear water. March through April is the best time to fish for a trophy.

Specks (crappie) between 8 and 10 inches are common in Frederick. The area around the pier and dam are best. Use jigs and minnows.

Channel catfish up to 30 pounds are taken from Frederick. Cut bait, crawlers, and prepared baits fished on the bottom at night are best.

Some large walleyes are taken. Biologists sampling the lake caught fish up to 9 pounds. Most were in the 2-to-3-pound range. This species will hit year-round, but the fish slow down in the winter. A spinner with a trailing night crawler trolled works really well. Try different depths until fish are found.

The best baits to use here, unless indicated otherwise above, are spoons, jigs, plastics, spinners, surface lures, crank baits, night crawlers, crawfish, and live minnows.

Access: A paved boat ramp and gravel parking lot are available.

For more information: VDGIF, 1320 Belman Rd., Fredericksburg, VA 22401; (540) 899–4169; www.dgif.virginia.gov/fishing/. Frederick County Chamber of Commerce, 2 N. Cameron St., Suite 200, Winchester, VA 22601; (540) 662–4118; www.winchesterva.org.

27 Burke Lake

Key species: Largemouth bass, musky, walleye, crappie, channel catfish, bluegill.

Best time to fish: All year.

Directions: From the Capital Beltway, take Interstate 95 to Woodbridge, then Route 123 (Ox Road) north to the lake.

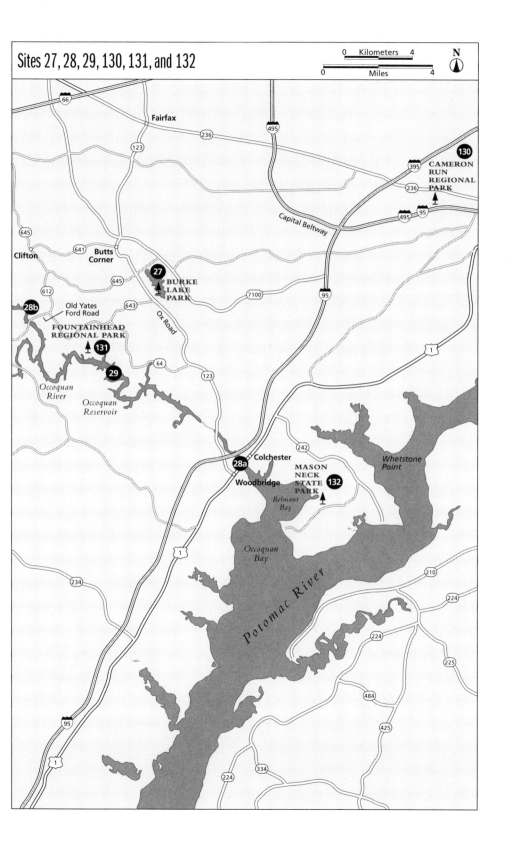

Sites 27, 28, 29, 130, 131, and 132

Description: This lake of more than 200 acres is owned by the Virginia Department of Game and Inland Fisheries (VDGIF). It is part of Fairfax County's Burke Lake Park. Since it is so close to a high-population center, it is heavily fished.

The fishing: Burke provides trophy musky every year. A good population of fish in the 20-to-25-pound class provide the action. Many cast or troll large spinners with big bucktails on the hook.

Big largemouths are also abundant. They can be difficult to catch because of the pressure. Crank and jerk baits are effective.

Lots of walleye in the 4-to-7-pound range are caught in this lake. Biologists have sampled fish over 9 pounds. Plastic grubs bounced on the bottom appear to work well. In the summer fish at night.

Channel cats, crappie, and bluegills are also abundant and good-sized.

The best baits for this area are minnows, shad, night crawlers, cut bait, spoons, big swimming lures, plastic jerk baits, and crank baits.

Special regulations: No gasoline engines. Electric trolling motors okay. No wading or swimming. Check all regulations, musky and bass in particular.

Access: There's a VDGIF concrete ramp. To reach it from the city of Fairfax, take Route 123 south to lake. Access is also available via the Burke Lake Park ramp, for which a fee applies. A nice wheelchair-accessible fishing pier can be reached from the VDGIF ramp parking lot. There's also a lighted wheelchair-accessible pier in the park (park entrance fee applies).

For more information: VDGIF, 1320 Belman Rd., Fredericksburg, VA 22401; (540) 899–4169; www.dgif.virginia.gov/fishing/. Burke Lake Park, 7315 Ox Rd., Fairfax Station, VA 22039, (703) 323–6601.

28 The Occoquan River *(see map on page 55)*

Key species: White perch, striped bass, largemouth bass, crappie, yellow perch, flathead catfish, channel catfish. Herring and shad in the spring.

Best time to fish: March through November.

Directions: The Occoquan is located in northern Virginia. It partially forms the border between Fairfax and Prince William Counties. To reach the lower portion of the river take either Interstate 95 or Route 1 south from Washington, D.C.

Description: This river is a tributary of the Potomac. It empties into Occoquan Bay, which in turn opens up into the Potomac.

The fishing: The lower portion of the river is tidal and has excellent fishing for white perch, stripers, and large channel and flathead cats. Be sure to know the regulations on striped bass. The best baits to use here are worms, grass shrimp, cut bait, spoons, small jigs, and plastics.

Fly patterns: Caddis larvae, stone flies, and various mayflies. Streamers and flashy marabous also work at times. Small poppers and bream busters.

Access: There's a boat ramp off Route 1 near Colchester (28a). To reach the boat ramp at Bull Run Marina Regional Park (28b), exit Interstate 66 at Fairfax and go south on Route 123 to Route 645 (Clifton Road). Take Route 645 west to Route 612 (Henderson Road). Go south on Route 612, then right on Old Yates Ford Road.

For more information: Virginia Department of Game and Inland Fisheries (VDGIF), 320 Belman Rd., Fredericksburg, VA 22401; (540) 899–4169; www.dgif.virginia.gov/fishing/. Virginia Marine Resources Commission, 2600 Washington Ave., Third Floor, Newport News, VA 23607; (757) 247–2200 or (757) 247–2292; www.mrc.state.va.us.

For the main stem of the Potomac River, check out the Potomac River Fisheries Commission Building, 222 Taylor St., P.O. Box 9, Colonial Beach, VA 22443; (804) 224–7148 or (800) 266–3904; www.prfc.state.va.us.

29 Occoquan Reservoir *(see map on page 55)*

Key species: Largemouth bass, crappie, channel and flathead catfish, bluegill.

Best time to fish: All year.

Directions: See individual parks.

Description: This reservoir is in close proximity to the D.C. metro area. It is a water-supply lake for the city of Fairfax and quite large, at 2,100 acres. This is a great place to introduce kids to fishing.

The fishing: Largemouth-bass fishing in Occoquan is excellent. A big population calls this lake its home. Four-to-six-pound fish are common and quite a few larger specimens are taken every year. This species can be difficult to catch because of the pressure and ample forage. Most use crank baits, plastic worms, and spinner baits.

Crappie fishing is also very good in the Occoquan. Both the white and black species are available. Fish around brush with small plastic jigs tipped with a minnow. When a fish is caught, fish the area thoroughly before moving on because these guys tend to hang out in large groups.

Channel and flathead cats provide good action in this lake. The state record flathead, 66 pounds, 4 ounces, was caught here in 1994. Fish rocky areas near steep drop-offs with live bait—sunfish are a favorite. The channels can be caught almost anywhere. They average about 14 inches.

Bluegill fishing is also good. Most are between 5 and 7 inches.

The best baits to use here are minnows, shad, night crawlers, cut bait, spoons, plastic jigs, and crank baits.

Special regulations: No engines larger than 9.9 horsepower. Check regulations for bass and pike.

Access: Boats can be rented from Fountainhead Regional Park off Interstate 95 south of the Capital Beltway. To get there, exit at Route 123 north and turn left (west) onto Hampton Road to park.

To reach Bull Run Marina Regional Park, exit Interstate 66 at Fairfax and go south on Route 123 to Route 645 (Clifton Road). Take Route 645 west to Route 612 (Henderson Road). Go south on Route 612, then right Old Yates Ford Road.

Boats can also be rented at Lake Ridge Park. From I–95, take Route 123 north to Old Bridge Road. Go west on Old Bridge Road to Hedges Run Road. Take Hedges Run Road north to Cotton Mill Drive. Go left on Cotton Mill Drive and take it into the park.

There's also a wheelchair-accessible fishing pier at Fountainhead Regional Park.

For more information: Northern Virginia Regional Park Authority Headquarters, 5400 Ox Rd., Fairfax Station, VA 22039; (703) 352–5900; www.nvrpa.org/fishing.html. Lake Ridge Park, Prince William County Park Authority, 12350 Cotton Mill Dr., Woodbridge, VA 22192; (703) 494–5288; www.pwcparks.org/lrpark. Virginia Department of Game and Inland Fisheries (VDGIF), 1320 Belman Rd., Fredericksburg, VA 22401; (540) 899–4169; www.dgif.virginia.gov/fishing/.

30 Lake Brittle

Key species: Largemouth bass, crappie, sunfish, walleye, channel catfish.

Best time to fish: All year.

Directions: From New Baltimore, take Route 29 east to Route 600 south (Broad Run Church Road) to Route 676 west to the lake.

Description: Lake Brittle is owned by the Virginia Department of Game and Inland Fisheries (VDGIF). It covers about 75 acres. It's a great place for a picnic and nature-watching. Gasoline engines are prohibited. Many people fish the shoreline at Brittle. A concession at the lake rents boats and sells bait.

The fishing: Most anglers try for redears and bluegill. The latter have been stunted recently because of the gizzard shad population.

Largemouth bass are in good shape in this lake, with some attaining weights of 6 pounds.

Channel cats average about 2 pounds, and a large population of small brown bullheads occupies the lake. Anglers are encouraged to release flathead cats because they tend to control the populations of stunted species.

The best live baits to use here are minnows and night crawlers. The best artificials are plastics, jigs, surface and swimming lures, and flies for sunfish, crappie, and bass.

Special regulations: Check all regulations with the VDGIF.

Access: A boat ramp and fishing pier are available.

For more information: VDGIF, 1320 Belman Rd., Fredericksburg, VA 22401; (540) 899–4169; www.dgif.virginia.gov/fishing/. Fauquier County Parks and Recreation, Vint Hill Village Green Community Center, Harrison Road, P.O. Box 861435, Warrenton, VA 20186; (540) 347–6894; www.fauquiercounty.gov/government/departments/parksrec/.

31 The North Fork of the Shenandoah River

Key species: Small and largemouth bass, catfish, panfish, crappie.

Best time to fish: All year.

Directions: Southwest of Timberville, Routes 259 and 789 (Strooptown Road) follow the North Fork. Continuing east out of the town on Route 211, make a left (north) onto Plains Mill Road, which becomes River Road. This follows the river for a distance. North of Mount Jackson, Red Banks Road parallels the river for a ways. From Edinburg to Strasburg, the river zigzags a lot and many of the roads that intersect Route 11 cross the North Folk. You'll need a detailed road atlas to access this river. The roads are too many to show on this map.

Description: Beautiful scenery, plenty of fish, clear water, and lots of wildlife make the North Fork of the Shenandoah an ideal stream to float in a canoe. At times the river is rather shallow and canoeists may have to walk their boats. Two low bridges and six dams have to be dealt with in a float of the entire river. Heading downstream, a dam is first encountered upstream of Timberville, then three more dams appear between Edinburg and the Route 758 bridge east of Woodstock. Two more small ones are found between Strasburg and Riverton.

This river begins in the mountains of Alleghany County and flows over a 100 miles to Front Royal, where it joins the South Fork and becomes the mainstream Shenandoah.

The fishing: Smallmouth bass is the primary species that anglers seek in the North Fork. According to the Virginia Department of Game and Inland Fisheries (VDGIF), the catch rate is very high, with experienced anglers catching as many as fifty a day.

Bluegills, redear, rock bass, and pumpkinseeds are all available in the North Fork. Fly-fishing for these species can provide some great sport. Mosquito patterns as well as bream busters work well.

Eels, suckers, carp, crappie, bullhead, and channel cats are also available.

The best baits to use here are night crawlers, crawdads, live minnows or leeches, and minnow-imitating artificials and plastics. Popping surface plugs are best for bass.

Fly patterns: Any pattern that looks like a minnow, crawfish or leech, and poppers.

Access: There are several VDGIF access points, including Meems Bottom (31a), which can be reached from Mount Jackson by taking Route 11 south to Route 730 west (Caverns Road). This crosses the river. There's a carry-into launch area.

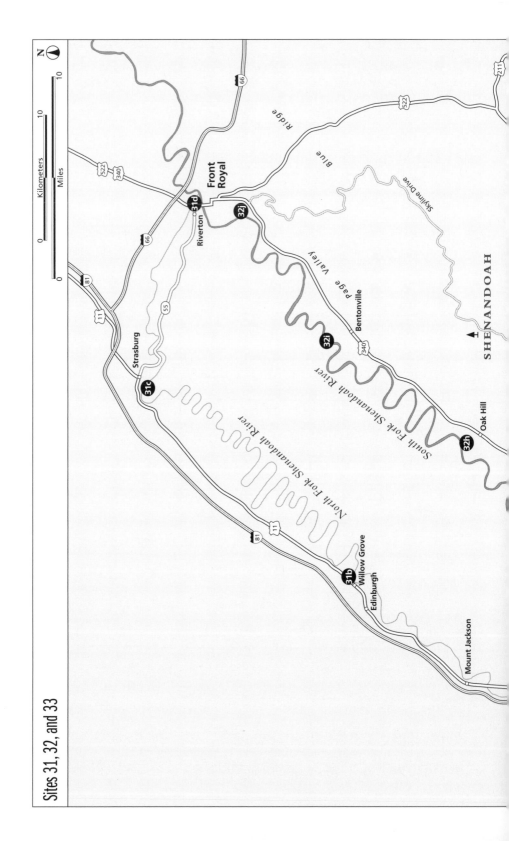

Sites 31, 32, and 33

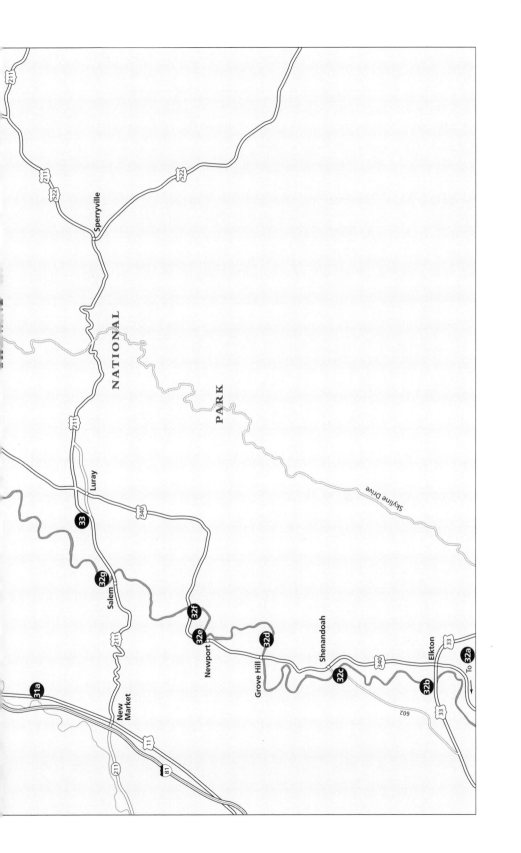

Another is near Willow Grove, reached via Route 11 north from Edinburg. Turn east onto Route 672 (Chapman's Landing Road) to a good boat ramp (31b).

Strasburg Town Park off of Route 55 also has a good ramp (31c).

For the Riverton access point, take Route 340/522 north out of Front Royal through Riverton to Route 637 (Guard Hill Road) to find a canoe access (31d).

For more information: VDGIF, 517 Lee Hwy., Verona, VA 24482; (540) 248–9360; fax (540) 248–9399; www.dgif.virginia.gov/fishing/. Shenandoah County Chamber of Commerce, (540) 459–2542. Front Royal–Warren County Chamber of Commerce, 104 E. Main St., Front Royal, VA 22630; (540) 635–3185; www.frontroyalchamber.com. For river conditions, contact the United States Geological Survey at (804) 261–2600 (www.usgs.gov).

32 The South Fork of the Shenandoah River *(see map on pages 60–61)*

Key species: Small and largemouth bass, catfish, panfish, crappie.

Best time to fish: All year.

Directions: This river meanders over a large portion of northwestern Virginia. Below find just a few places where it can be accessed.

From Island Ford, take Route 640 west, which crosses Captain Yancey Road (Route 642). This road runs along the east bank for a distance in each direction. Continuing across the South Fork, Power Dam Road runs south along the west bank. (Not on map.)

From Grove Hill follow Route 340 north to Route 650 (Grove Hill River Road). This parallels the river for a few miles.

From Luray, take Route 675 (Bixlers Ferry Road) across the South Fork. Turn north on Route 684 (South Page Valley Road). This route periodically follows and then moves away from the river for a long distance.

Description: Though the South Fork of the Shenandoah River produces some Class I and II rapids, it is very popular with canoeists. It flows for about 100 miles beginning near Port Republic and converges with the North Fork of the Shenandoah River at Front Royal to form the main stem of the Shenandoah. It averages about 100 feet in width and may become clogged with vegetation in areas during the warm months. Dams on this river are found at Shenandoah, Newport, and Luray.

The South Fork is very scenic and becomes relatively crowded during nice weather.

The fishing: The South Fork is an excellent river for smallmouth bass. While it is not known for trophies, experienced anglers can catch as many as fifty to seventy-five fish in a day.

Panfish, bluegills, rock bass, and pumpkinseeds are all available in the South Fork. The most abundant sunfish is the redbreast and 6-to-8-inch specimens are common. Fly-fishing for these species can provide some great sport. Mosquito patterns as well as bream busters work well.

Crappie are found in the larger pools. Use small jigs with small minnows for bait.

Catfish are found throughout the river with 2-pound-plus channels very common. Fish the larger pools.

Though not targeted by many, a good population of bucket mouths resides in the South Fork. As with everywhere else, fish the slow pools and brush piles.

The Virginia Department of Game and Inland Fisheries (VDGIF) stocks fingerling muskies yearly. The population of this species is small, but they can be a worthwhile pursuit.

Eels, suckers, carp, crappie, bullhead, and channel cats are also available.

The best baits to use in this area, unless otherwise indicated above, are night crawlers, crawdads, live minnows or leeches, and minnow-imitating artificials and plastics. Popping surface plugs are best for bass.

Special regulations: Bass regulations are different in various areas. Check them out before fishing.

Fly patterns: Any pattern that looks like a minnow, crawfish or leech, and poppers. Deer-hair bass bugs.

Access: Over twenty access areas are found along the South Fork. Just a few are described here. Not all roads are drawn on the map. A detailed atlas is required.

There's a VDGIF access point at Port Republic on Route 659 (32a).

There's also one near Elkton. From Route 340, turn west onto Route 33 and follow it to the bridge (32b).

In Shenandoah turn southwest onto Commertown Road (Route 602) to reach the VDGIF access point (32c), which is located near the hydro dam by the bridge.

In Grove Hill turn east on Route 650 to the VDGIF ramp (32d).

In Newport go north on Route 340 (32e).

To reach the ramp in Alma, turn east toward the town off Route 340 and cross the bridge to the east bank. The ramp is below (32f).

For the Salem ramp, take Route 211 west from Luray. After crossing the river, turn onto Route 646 to the ramp (32g).

Take Route 675 west across the river to the Luray access point.

To reach the Oak Hill ramp, from Route 340 take Cavalier Road (Route 661) west to the ramp (32h).

From Front Royal, take Route 340 south to Route 613 west and cross the river to reach the Bentonville ramp (32i).

To get to the Front Royal access point, take Mountain Road (Route 677) west from Route 340. The ramp is located before the bridge (32j).

Camping: Shenandoah River State Park, P.O. Box 235, Daughter of Stars Drive, Bentonville, VA 22610; (540) 622–6840 or (800) 933–PARK; www.dcr.state.va.us/parks/andygues.htm.

For more information: VDGIF, 517 Lee Hwy., Verona, VA 24482; (540) 248–9360; www.dgif.virginia.gov/fishing/. Shenandoah County Chamber of Commerce, (540)

459–2542. Front Royal–Warren County Chamber of Commerce, (540) 635–3185; www.frontroyalchamber.com. For river conditions, contact the United States Geological Survey at (804) 261–2600 (www.usgs.gov).

33 Arrowhead Lake *(see map on pages 60–61)*

Key species: Largemouth bass, bluegill, redear sunfish, catfish, walleye.

Best time to fish: March through November.

Directions: From Luray, take Fairview Road 4 miles southeast to Lake Arrowhead Road.

Description: Arrowhead Lake covers about 40 acres and is in the Arrowhead Recreation Area, which is run by the town of Luray. It is a delightful place to spend an afternoon fishing with the family. Anglers can fish from most of the lake's shoreline.

The fishing: This lake has a lot of bass under 11 inches. Anglers are encouraged to take these smaller fish. Anglers should concentrate on structure—downed trees, beaver lodges, and weed beds.

Plenty of sunfish, redear, and bluegills populate Lake Arrowhead. In recent years the average size has increased.

Seven-to-nine-inch crappie are common. Fish the same areas as for bass. Walleye and northern pike are stocked annually by Virginia Department of Game and Inland Fisheries (VDGIF). The populations are small but worth fishing for. Channel cats do well in Arrowhead. Some 20-pounders are caught most years. The VDGIF stocks this species annually to maintain the population.

The best baits to use for cats are minnows, night crawlers, and cut bait. Plastics, surface lures, and flies are best for sunfish and bass.

Special regulations: A permit from the Town of Luray is required. A small fee applies. Check bass regulations.

Access: The park has a concrete ramp.

For more information: VDGIF, 127 Lee Hwy., P.O. Box 996, Verona, VA 24482; (540) 248–9360; www.dgif.virginia.gov/fishing/. Town of Luray, 45 E. Main St., Luray, VA 22385; (540) 743–5511. Visitor Information Center, 46 E. Main St., Luray, VA 22835; (540) 743–3915, (540) 743–4530, or (888) 743–3915; http://luray page.com/moreattractions.htm.

34 Leesylvania State Park

Key species: Smallmouth and striped bass, catfish.

Best time to fish: Early spring through autumn.

Directions: From Interstate 95, take Route 638 (Blackburn Road) east to Route 1

You might tangle with an eel at Leesylvania State Park.

south and turn east onto Nabasco Road. Follow it to the park entrance. Alternatively, take the Cardinal Drive (Route 610) exit east off I-95. Cross Route 1 where it becomes Nabasco Road and follow it to the park entrance.

Description: Leesylvania is close to the D.C. metropolitan area and is a very popular destination, especially on nice holiday weekends. It has just about everything, including picnic areas, playgrounds, and hiking trails. The park is on the shores of the Potomac River. Fees apply.

The fishing: Fishing for blue and channel cats is excellent. The bulkheads, decks and rock barriers, and jetties are great habitat for smallies. Bank angling is very popular, with most anglers casting bottom rigs.

The best baits to use here are night crawlers, cut bait, live minnows, plastics, and swimming lures.

Special regulations: The Potomac River Commission sets the regulations for this area of the river. Be sure to have an up-to-date copy of their information.

Access: A very large boat ramp is located at the park. A separate canoe/car-top launch is also available. A boat-storage facility (fee charged) is also present for those who do not want to drag their trailers. The park also has a nice fishing pier.

For more information: Potomac River Fisheries Commission, 222 Taylor St., P.O. Box 9, Colonial Beach, VA 22443; (804) 224–7148 or (800) 266–3904; www.prfc.state.va.us. Leesylvania State Park, 2001 Daniel K. Ludwig Dr., Woodbridge, VA 22191-4504; (703) 670–0372; www.dcr.virginia.gov/state_parks/lee.shtml.

35 The Upper Rappahannock River

Key species: Smallmouth bass, redbreast sunfish, catfish.

Best time to fish: February through November.

Directions: To reach the Upper Rappahannock, take Interstate 95 south out of Washington, D.C. and northern Virginia. It crosses the river near Fredericksburg. Follow directions below to individual accesses.

Description: From Chester Gap in Fauquier County, the Rappahannock flows over 180 miles before emptying into the Chesapeake Bay. For this book, the Upper Rappahannock is defined as the headwaters to tidewater that is at Fredericksburg. The landscape along its banks varies from forest to agricultural to urban. Above the intersections of the Rapidan and Hazel Rivers, the water is crystal clean. Below it could be muddy because of erosion from those two tributaries.

The fishing: Smallmouth-bass fishing is excellent in the upper river. This water was made for these fighters. Anglers can also try for catfish and redbreast sunfish.

The best baits to use here are night crawlers, crawdads, and live minnows or leeches. Minnow-imitating artificials and plastics are also good.

Fly patterns: Any pattern that looks like a minnow, crawfish, or leech.

Access: Most of the access points are primitive, suitable for canoes or small johnboats.

Kelly's Ford is located on Route 672 off Route 651 (35a). To reach Motts Landing from Interstate 95 outside of Fredericksburg, exit onto Bragg Road (Route 639) west. Turn right (west) onto Route 618 (River Road) and follow it to the ramp (35b). It is a long float to the next access point: about 25 miles. Plan on an overnight camp. On the Rapidan River, which flows into the Rappahannock, there's a canoe access point at Eleys Ford Road (Route 610) southeast of Richardsville (35c).

This drift is for the experienced only. The sites at bridges crossing the river are undeveloped. A few private launch sites are available. Contact Clore Brothers (540–786–7749) or Rappahannock Outdoor Education Center (540–371–5085).

Camping: Rappahannock River Campground, Richardsville, VA 22736-2018; (540) 399–1839 or (800) 784-PADL; www.canoecamp.com.

Outfitters include Clore Brothers Outfitters, 5927 River Rd., Fredericksburg, VA 22407, (540) 786–7749 or (540) 786–7456, www.clorebros.com, and Outdoor Adventures/The Rappahannock Angler, 4721 Plank Rd., Fredericksburg, VA 22407, (540) 786–3334, www.outdooradventures.net.

Sites 35, 36, and 38

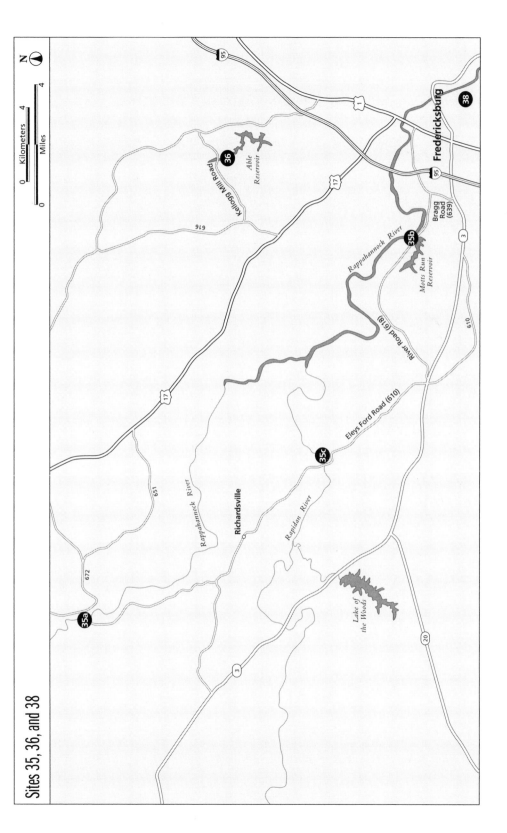

Kellogg Mill Road

Able Reservoir

36

616

17

Rappahannock River

35b

Motts Run Reservoir

Bragg Road (639)

River Road (618)

Eleys Ford Road (610)

35c

610

610

3

95

1

95

Fredericksburg

38

3

651

Rappahannock River

672

Richardsville

Rapidan River

35a

3

Lake of the Woods

20

N

0 Kilometers 4

0 Miles 4

This Web site describes a number of float trips on the Rappahannock: www
.dgif.virginia.gov/fishing/waterbodies/display.asp?id=170&section=maps.

For more information: Friends of the Rappahannock, P.O. Box 7254, Fredericksburg, VA 22404; (540) 373–3448; www.riverfriends.org. Virginia Outdoor Cen-
ter/Rappahannock Outdoor Education Center, 3219 Fall Hill Ave., Fredericksburg,
VA 22401; (540) 371–5085 or (877) PLAY–VA2; www.playva.com/rec.

36 Abel Reservoir (Safford County Reservoir) *(see map on page 67)*

Key species: Largemouth bass, crappie, bluegills, pickerel, catfish.

Best time to fish: April through November.

Directions: From Fredericksburg, take Warrenton Road (Route 17) north, then take
a right on Poplar Road (Route 616). Make a right (south) onto Kellogg Mill Road,
then a left (east) before the bridge for parking.

Description: Abel's surface area is about 170 acres and surrounded by very steep
embankments and rocks. Only electric motors are allowed. Clean the prop of your
engine before putting it into other lakes as hydrilla is present.

The fishing: There is not much structure in Abel, and it is home to some very large
bass. Large pickerel and fine crappie angling are available. Excellent channel catfish
and bluegill populations are also present.

   The best baits to use here are spinner baits, jigs, plastics, spoons, spinners, surface lures, night crawlers, and live minnows.

Access: A boat ramp with parking is available.

For more information: Stafford County Parks and Recreation Department, (540)
752–5632; http://stafford.va.us/parks/parks_&_places/index.shtml.

37 Lake Orange

Key species: Largemouth bass, crappie, channel cats.

Best time to fish: March through November.

Directions: Travel east on Route 20 out of Orange. Then turn right (south) on
Route 629 and left (east) on Route 739 to the lake and ramp.

Description: If you want to fish surrounded by bucolic scenery, this 125-acre lake
owned by Virginia Department of Game and Inland Fisheries (VDGIF) is the place to
choose. The area behind the shoreline is a mixture of gently slopping farmland and
hardwood forests. Trolling motors are allowed but gasoline engines are not. Picnic
tables and shelters are available. Boat rentals and bait and tackle are also sold at the lake.

The fishing: Bucket mouths in the 12-to-15-inch category abound, and to make
things interesting, 15-to-20-inch fish are common. Most consider this a good large-

mouth lake. These fish are not always easy to catch because plenty of forage, particularly gizzard shad, are available. Lures imitating this species are best.

Lake Orange supports a good population of walleye. Four- and five-pounders are caught every year. Try trolling crawlers or minnows behind spinners. Vary the depth until you find fish.

Plenty of channel catfish in the 1-to-3-pound class swim the waters of Lake Orange. Some cast off the bank and fish the bottom at night with fish-finder rigs.

The best baits to use here are plastics, spinners, crank baits, and other swimming plugs, plus live minnows and night crawlers.

Black crappie and bluegill panfish are also abundant. The gills are on the small side, but the crappie average about 8 inches with many in the 13-to-15-inch category. Use worms for the sunfish and small jigs, bucktail, or plastic, tipped with minnows, for the specks.

Fly patterns: Bass bugs and poppers. Mosquitoes and bream busters.

Access: The VDGIF has developed a barrier-free boat ramp and fishing pier.

Cottages and B&Bs: The Vineyard Cottage, Barboursville Vineyards, 17655 Winery Rd., Barboursville, VA 22923; (540) 832–7848; www.palladiorestaurant.com/cottage .html. Willow Grove Inn, 14079 Plantation Way, Orange, VA 22960; (540) 672–5982 or (800) 949–1778; www.willowgroveinn.com.

For more information: VDGIF, 1320 Belman Rd., Fredericksburg, VA 22401; (540) 899–4169; www.dgif.virginia.gov/fishing/. Angler's Landing at Lake Orange, 20281 Lake Orange Rd., Orange, VA 22960; (540) 672-3997; www.visitocva.com/ lake%20orange.htm. Department of Tourism and Visitors Bureau, 122 E. Main St., Orange, VA 22960; (540) 672–1653 or (877) 222–8072.

38 The Lower Rappahannock River

Key species: Striped bass, shad, largemouth bass, catfish.

Best time to fish: March through October.

Directions: See Access below.

Description: The Lower Rappahannock is defined as the area of the river that is tidal. This is from Fredericksburg to the Chesapeake Bay. Embrey Dam was removed as an obstruction. Now the river is open above Fredericksburg for anadromous species.

The fishing: The former Embrey Dam in Fredericksburg is the site of a large shad-and-herring run each spring. Many say the time to fish is two weeks on either side of Easter. Most cast shad darts or just plain gold hooks for these mini-tarpon. The lower river also has a large run of white perch and good fishing for largemouth bass, crappie, yellow perch, and very large blue catfish. Stripers are abundant in the tidal Rappahannock.

The best baits to use in this area are live minnows, crawlers, cut bait, and commercial catfish bait, plus minnow-imitating artificials, plastics, and shad darts for shad.

Fly patterns: Any pattern that looks like a minnow, shad or herring.

Access: The Virginia Department of Game and Inland Fisheries (VDGIF) maintains a barrier-free ramp at the Fredericksburg City Docks on Sophia Street. The VDGIF also maintains Carter's Wharf, which is reached by following Route 3 west from Warsaw, turning north onto Route 624, and then east (left) onto Route 622. A third VDGIF access point is Simonson Landing. From Farnham, go southeast on Route 3 and turn southwest onto Route 608, then south on Route 606 to the ramp.

For more information: Friends of the Rappahannock, P.O. Box 7254, Fredericksburg, VA 22404; (540) 373–3448; www.riverfriends.org. Virginia Outdoor Center/Rappahannock Outdoor Education Center, 3219 Fall Hill Ave., Fredericksburg, VA 22401; (540) 371–5085 or (877) PLAY–VA2; www.playva.com/rec. VDGIF, 1320 Belman Rd., Fredericksburg, VA 22401; (540) 899–4169; www.dgif.virginia .gov/fishing/.

Outfitters include Clore Brothers Outfitters, 5927 River Rd., Fredericksburg, VA 22407, (540) 786–7749 or (540) 786–7456, www.clorebros.com, and Outdoor Adventures/The Rappahannock Angler, 4721 Plank Rd., Fredericksburg, VA 22407, (540) 786–3334, www.outdooradventures.net.

39 Lake Gordonsville (Bowlers Mill)

Key species: Largemouth bass, crappie, catfish.

Best time to fish: April through November.

Directions: From Charlottesville, take Interstate 64 east, then Route 15 north. Turn west on Route 603 and follow it to the lake.

Description: This lake, owned by the Louisa County Parks and Recreation Department, covers 75 acres. Gordonsville is very popular and gets quite crowded, especially on weekends. A permit is required from the Louisa County Water Department, and gasoline engines are prohibited.

The fishing: This small lake is packed full of bigmouths. Many are over 20 inches. Weedless plastics work really well around the abundant weed beds.

The best baits to use in this area are jigs, plastics, and surface lures, night crawlers, commercial catfish bait, and live minnows.

Access: This area has a gravel boat ramp.

Camping: KOA Charlottesville, Charlottesville; (804) 296–9881; www.koa .com/where/va/46103/index.htm. Misty Mountain Camp Resort, Charlottesville; (888) 647–8900; www.mistycamp.com. Christopher Run Campground, Mineral;

(540) 894–4744; www.christopherruncampground.com. Small Country Camp-ground, Louisa; (540) 967–2431; www.smallcountry.com.

For more information: Fishing permits are available at the Louisa County Treasurer's Office (540–967–3435), Carterfields Sporting Supply (540–967–1220), and Gordonsville Sports Supply (540–832–7013). Louisa County Parks and Recreation Department, http://louweb.louisa.org/parks/facilities.asp#parks. Virginia Department of Game and Inland Fisheries (VDGIF), 1320 Belman Rd., Fredericksburg, VA 22401; (540) 899–4169; www.dgif.virginia.gov/fishing/.

40 Lake Anna

Key species: Largemouth bass, bluegill, redear sunfish, striped bass, channel catfish, walleye.

Best time to fish: March through November, but good fishing can also be had all winter long.

Directions: Take Interstate 95 south out of Fredericksburg. Go west on Route 208 to the lake.

Description: Lake Anna is a large man-made lake that was impounded in 1972. Since that time there have been many stockings and most species are self-sustaining. There are a number of towns in the area, and facilities are available nearby.

The fishing: Lake Anna is one of the finest largemouth-bass locations in Virginia and is among the top waters for trophy-sized lunkers. Plenty of fish in the 4-to-6-pound range are taken every year. Since it is a reasonable distance from some northern Virginia metropolitan areas, this body of water receives a lot of fishing pressure. Because of this, any angler needs persistence and patience to consistently catch fish. Bass anglers should have a big variety of lures and try as many different habitats as possible.

Because of a lack of well-oxygenated, cool water, striped bass do not do too well in Lake Anna. However, they do grow well for a few years and attain the 20-inch minimum size. This population is maintained by annual stocking. The best fishing for this species in Lake Anna is during the winter. The cold months find the stripers chasing bait near the surface. Some of the best lures are sassy shads and bucktails. Many also use live gizzard shad or blueback herring.

Lake Anna has a very healthy population of channel cats. They are numerous and range from 14 to 20 inches and average about 3 pounds. Most use a fish-finder rig, that is, a slip-sinker with a leadered hook tied to a swivel. The favorite baits are live shiners, night crawlers, cut bait (herring, shrimp), or commercial dough baits. Chicken livers are also often used. Some very large channel cats have been documented in Lake Anna by biologists. A state or even world record may be caught here soon. Beside the channel catties, white catfish, bullheads, and even a few blue catfish are present.

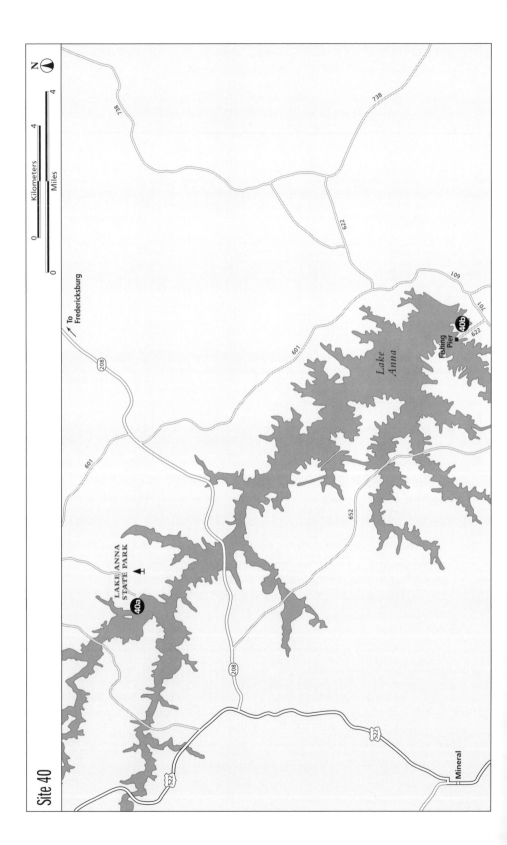

Site 40

The walleye population in Lake Anna is maintained by annual stocking. Most are caught in the Pamunkey River arm of the lake from February through April. The fish are found along the red-clay banks and drop-offs from the old Virginia Department of Game and Inland Fisheries (VDGIF) boat ramp downstream to Terry's Run. Most of these fish are taken on spinning gear loaded with plastic grubs or bucktails. However, live bait such as minnows, leeches, and night crawlers are also used effectively.

There are a number panfish species in Lake Anna. One of the favorites is the black crappie. They grow to a respectable size in this body of water. Many 2- and 3-pounders are taken each year. These guys are minnow feeders and as such, live bait, jigs, and small spinners and spoons all work well. Look for crappie around brush piles, docks, and other obstructions. March through May is the best time to go after these guys.

Respectable populations of white perch and various sunfish species are found in this lake. They are available throughout the year, and most people use small grubs or worms for bait.

The best baits to use, unless otherwise specified above, are minnows, night crawlers, shad, crank baits, plastics, and surface lures.

Many tournaments take place on Lake Anna. Some originate at the Sturgeon Creek Marina. For more information, call (540) 895–5095 or visit www.sturgeon creekmarina.com/tournaments.htm.

Access: There are numerous marinas and boat ramps at Lake Anna.

Anna Point Marina, 13721 Anna Point Lane, Mineral, VA 23667; (540) 895–5900.

Duke Creek Marina, 3831 Breaknock Rd., Spotsylvania, VA 22553; (540) 895–5065.

High Point Marina, 4634 Courthouse Rd., Mineral, VA 23117; (540) 895–5249.

Hunter's Landing, 6320 Belmont Rd., Mineral, VA 23117; (540) 854–5756.

Lake Anna Marina, (540) 895–5051.

Lake Anna State Park (40a), (540) 854–5503.

Rocky Branch Marina & Campground, (540) 895–5475.

Sturgeon Creek Marina, 4303 Boggs Dr., Bumpass, VA 23024; (540) 895–5095.

A wheelchair-accessible catwalk (40b) for anglers is found at Dike #3. From Route 208, turn south onto Route 601, then turn right (west) on Route 701 and right (north) onto Route 622. Alternately, from Route 208, take Route 652 south to Route 701 north to 622.

Camping: Lake Anna State Park, (540) 854–5503; www.dcr.state.va.us/parks/lake anna.htm. Rocky Branch Marina and Campground, Spotsylvania, VA 22553, (540) 895–5475; www.hikercentral.com/campgrounds/112539.html. Lake Anna Family Campground, 2983 New Bridge Rd., Mineral, VA 23112; (540) 894–9225. Christopher Run Campground, (540) 894–4744; www.christopherruncampground.com.

For more information: Louisa County Chamber of Commerce, (540) 967–0944; www.louisachamber.org/outside_frame.asp. Orange County Chamber of Commerce, (540) 672–5216; www.orangevachamber.com. Spotsylvania County Department of Tourism, (877) 515–6197; www.spotsylvania.va.us/departments/tourism/. VDGIF, 1320 Belman Rd., Fredericksburg, VA 22401; (540) 899–4169; www.dgif.virginia.gov/fishing/.

41 Gardy's Mill Pond

Key species: Largemouth bass, bluegill, redear sunfish.

Best time to fish: All year.

Directions: Take Route 202 northwest from Callao. Turn south onto Route 617 to the pond.

Description: This is a great place to get away from it all. It's rarely crowded and has some nice fish to boot.

The fishing: This place has some really nice-size bluegills and redears, some going over a pound. Recently some large bucket mouths have also been caught. Some of these were over 6 pounds.

The best baits to use here are night crawlers and minnows and swimming lures for bass.

Gardy's Mill Pond has a boat ramp and small pier.

Access: There's a Virginia Department of Game and Inland Fisheries (VDGIF) boat ramp and small parking area. A small pier for fishing is also available.

For more information: VDGIF, 5806 Mooretown Rd., Williamsburg, VA 23188; (757) 253–4172; www.dgif.virginia.gov/fishing/.

42 Chandler's Mill Pond

Key species: Largemouth bass, sunfish crappie, catfish.

Directions: Route 3 crosses the pond north of Montross.

Description: This pretty 75-acre pond is conveniently located off Route 3 in West-moreland County. It's a great place to take a kid fishing.

The fishing: The pond has an ample supply of crappie and sunfish. Better bass are now being caught there with some in the 4-pound range.

The best baits to use here are minnows, worms, and surface lures. The best flies are bass bugs.

Special regulations: Check bass regulations with the Virginia Department of Game and Inland Fisheries (VDGIF).

Access: A nice boat ramp and pier are available.

For more information: VDGIF, 5806 Mooretown Rd., Williamsburg, VA 23188; (757) 253–4172; www.dgif.virginia.gov/fishing/.

43 The Mattaponi River

Key species: White perch, yellow perch, blue catfish, striped bass.

Best time to fish: March through October.

Directions: From Richmond, take Route 360 northeast. It crosses the Mattaponi near the town of Aylett. Follow directions below to individual accesses.

Description: The Mattaponi is one of the two main sources for the York River. The Pamunkey is the other. It is one of the cleanest lowland rivers in the eastern United States and has very little development and agriculture along its banks.

The fishing: Yellow perch are featured in this river. Late winter (mid-February to mid-March) is the time to fish for trophy yellows. The best area is between Walkerton and Aylett. Minnows, worms, or plastic grubs are best.

White perch are found throughout the river. The tidal areas appear to hold more fish. Most people fish with bait, particularly grass shrimp if available.

Striped-bass fishing is excellent in the entire river all through the spring season but confined to the lower areas in autumn. Watch for spawning areas, which are closed to all fishing.

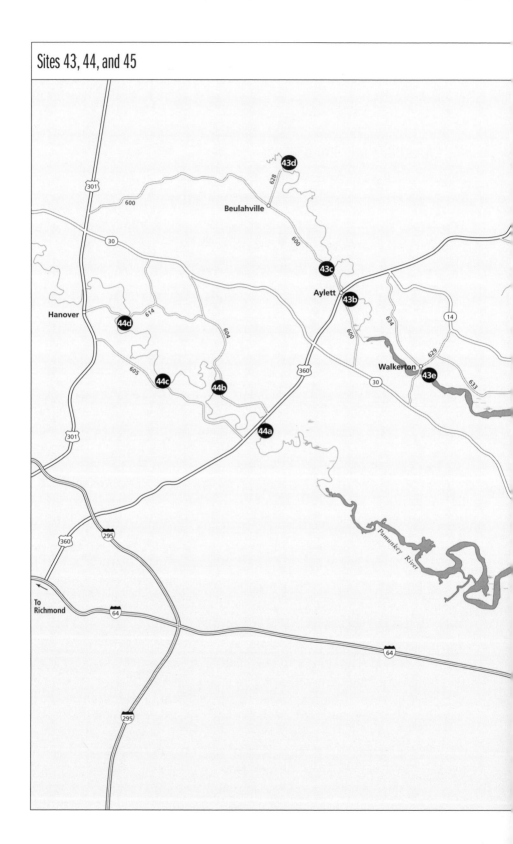

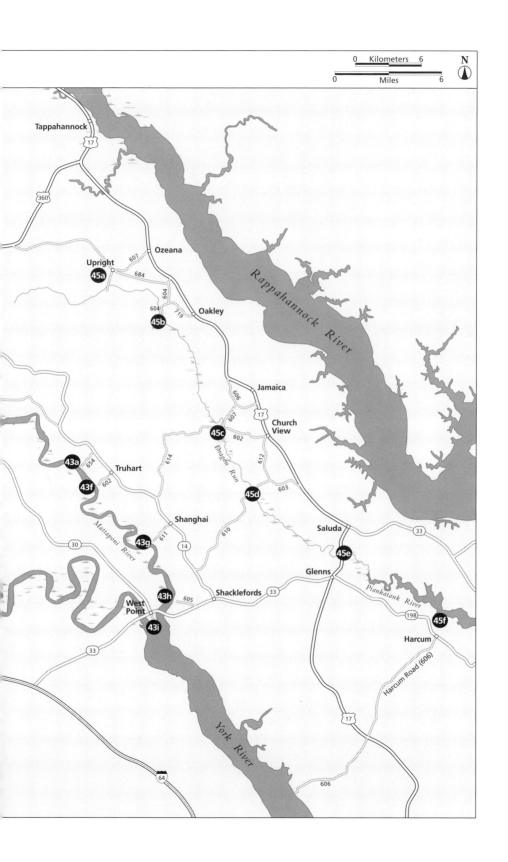

N

0   Kilometers   6
0   Miles   6

Tappahannock

17

360

Ozeana

Upright   607
45a
         684
              604

         604   Oakley
45b   719

              606   Jamaica
              607   17
                     Church
         602   View
45c
43a 654
         602   Truhart   614
43f   612
                    Dragon Run   603
         Shanghai   **45d**
43g 611   610   Saluda   33
         30   14   **45e**
                                 Glenns
43h   605   Shacklefords   33   Piankatank River
West   198
Point   **45f**
43i   Harcum

33   Harcum Road (606)

64   York River   17

                              606

Rappahannock River

Mattaponi River

Blue cats up to 20 pounds are common, with some topping as much as 30 pounds. The area around Walkerton is best. White and channel cats are also plentiful.

Above Aylett, the Mattaponi becomes a freshwater fishery with largemouth bass, crappie, and sunfish.

The best baits to use here are night crawlers, bloodworms, grass shrimp, cut bait, live minnows, swimming plugs, and jigs.

Special regulations: Check special regulations on anadromous striped bass. Regulations are set by the Virginia Marine Resources Commission (VMRC) (800–541–4646; www.mrc.state.va.us/regulations/regindex.shtm).

Access: A canoe and car-top boat access is located near Truhart (43a). To reach this access, take Route 14 north to Route 654, turn southwest, and follow it to the end. There is also one near Aylett (43c). Take West River Road (Route 600) north to just southeast of Millwood Road (Route 607). To reach the Beulahville access point (43d), take Dorrell Road (Route 628) north to the river.

Access points with ramps include one near Aylett, which can be reached from Route 360, by taking West River Road (Route 600) south a short distance to the ramp (43b). For the Walkerton ramp, take Walkerton Road (Route 629) from Route 14 southwest to the river (43e). For the ramp near Truhart, take Route 602 southwest from Route 14 to the river (43f). Near Shanghai, find the ramp by taing Route 611 southwest to the river (43g). For the ramp near Snow Hill, turn west off Route 33 onto Route 605 to the ramp (43h). There's also a ramp at West Point off Route 33 (43i).

For more information: Virginia Department of Game and Inland Fisheries (VDGIF), Chesapeake office, 3909 Airline Boulevard, Chesapeake, VA 23321; (757) 465-6811; www.dgif.virginia.gov/fishing/.

44 The Pamunkey River (see map on pages 76–77)

Key species: White perch, blue catfish, striped bass.

Best time to fish: March through October.

Directions: Take Route 301 north from Richmond. It crosses the Pamunkey just past the town of Hanover. Follow directions below to individual accesses.

Description: The Pamunkey is one of the two main sources for the York River. Mattaponi is the other. It is a really pretty river and a wonderful place to spend a day floating.

The fishing: White perch are found throughout the river. The lower areas appear to hold more fish during the spring and summer.

Striped-bass fishing is excellent throughout the river during the spring season but confined to the lower areas in autumn.

Blue cats up to 20 pounds are common, with some topping 45 pounds. The best area for these guys is a few miles on either side of Cumberland Marsh Natural Area Preserve. White and channel cats are also available.

Above White House the Pamunkey becomes a traditional warm freshwater fishery. Largemouth bass, crappie, and yellow perch dominate. Further upstream, north and west of where Route 360 crosses the river, redbreast sunfish and smallmouth begin to show up. Carp are also abundant in this area.

The best baits to use here are night crawlers, bloodworms, cut bait, and live minnows. Swimming plugs and jigs are best for stripers.

Special regulations: Check special regulations on anadromous striped bass. Regulations are set by the Virginia Marine Resources Commission (VMRC) (800–541–4646; www.mrc.state.va.us/regulations/regindex.shtm).

Access: Canoe and car-top boat accesses can be found at Route 360, right at the base of the bridge (44a); Dabneys Mill Road (Route 604), a bit south of where Landing Road tees with 604 (44b); Nelson's Bridge Road (44c), reached from Route 301 by turning east on Route 605, then north on Route 615; and Etna Mill Road (44d), reached from Route 301 by going east on Route 614/Norman's Bridge Road, which becomes Etna Mill Road.

A ramp is available at West Point off Route 30 (43i).

For more information: Virginia Department of Game and Inland Fisheries (VDGIF), Chesapeake office, 3909 Airline Boulevard, Chesapeake, VA 23321; (757) 465-6811; www.dgif.virginia.gov/fishing/.

45 The Piankatank River/Dragon Run (see map on pages 76-77)

Key species: Pickerel, white perch, redbreast sunfish, bowfin, striped bass.

Best time to fish: March through October.

Directions: The Piankatank runs parallel to and a bit south of the Rappahannock. The best way to access this river is by taking one of the numerous crossroads off Route 17, which also runs more-or-less parallel and northeast of the river. See the individual accesses below for details.

Description: The Piankatank runs out of Dragon Run, which is a beautiful cypress-lined stream. Upstream, black nontidal water dominates the Dragon. It becomes vegetation-choked in late spring, especially in the numerous side channels and swampy areas. Downstream, with the increased tidal influence, the lower river opens up a bit.

The fishing: Chain pickerel are a feature of this stream. Good-size specimens are caught every year. Nice-size redbreast sunfish and white perch provide good panfish action. In fact, this river system might be the best place in Virginia in which to fish for whities—many 12-inchers are caught here.

Largemouth bass, striped bass, channel catfish, hand-size bluegill, and carp round out the angling picture.

The best baits for this area are night crawlers, bloodworms, and live minnows, plus spoons, swimming plugs, jigs, spinners, and plastics.

Special regulations: Check special regulations on anadromous striped bass. Regulations are set by the Virginia Marine Resources Commission (VMRC) (800) 541–4646; www.mrc.state.va.us/regulations/regindex.shtm.

Access: Canoe and car-top boat access, with limited parking, is available near Upright. From Ozeana on Route 17, take 607 (Upright Road) west. This becomes Cheaneys Bridge Road, then Jones Bridge Road, but stays 607. Follow it to the river (45a).

Similar access is available at Byrds Bridge. From Oakley on Route 17, take Yorkers Swamp Road (Route 719) west. Turn left (southwest) on Route 604 (Byrds Bridge Road) and follow it to the river (45b).

To reach Dragon Road from Jamaica, take Route 17 south. Turn west on Route 606, then south on 607 (Dragon Road) and follow it to the river (45c).

For the Farley Park Road access point, from Route 17 at Church View, take Edgehill Road (Route 612) west to Farley Park Road (Route 603) and follow it to the river (45d).

In Saluda, canoes can be launched under the bridge where Route 17 crosses the Piankatank (45e).

A good boat ramp is located near Harcum. From Route 198, follow Harcum Road (Route 606) north and turn left (west) where it intersects Route 678. Continue on Route 606 to the end (45f).

For more information: Virginia Department of Game and Inland Fisheries (VDGIF), Chesapeake office, 3909 Airline Boulevard, Chesapeake, VA 23321 (757) 465-6811; www.dgif.virginia.gov/fishing/.

Southeastern Virginia

Southeastern Virginia consists mostly of low bottom lands. Slow-moving streams and quiet lakes are the norm. The angler will find everything from anadromous shad to large bucket mouths and giant catfish to test their skill.

46 Diascund Creek Reservoir

Key species: Largemouth bass, crappie, pickerel, bowfin, carp, white and yellow perch, redear, sunfish.

Best time to fish: All year.

Directions: From Providence Forge, take Route 60 east past Lanexa to Route 603 north. Follow it to the lake.

Description: This 1,100-acre reservoir is close to Williamsburg. It is a water-supply lake for the city of Newport News.

Diascund Creek Reservoir has an excellent population of largemouth bass.

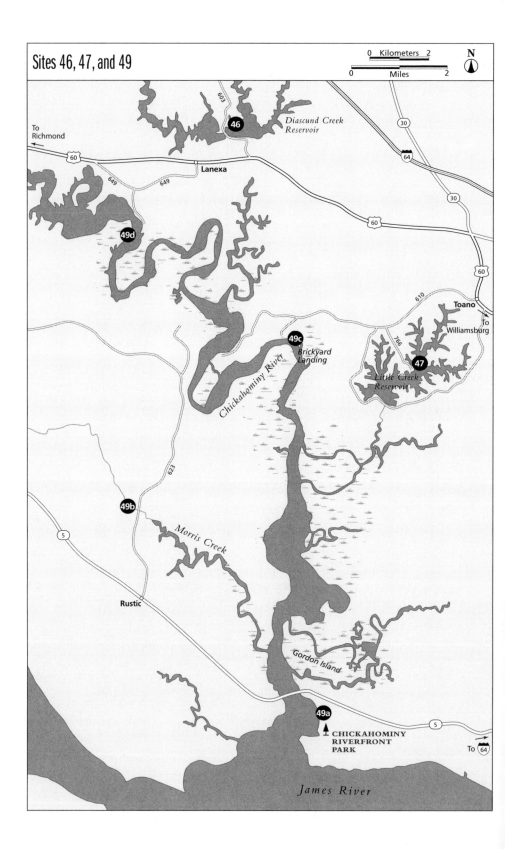

Sites 46, 47, and 49

0   Kilometers   2

0   Miles   2

N

To Richmond

Diascund Creek Reservoir

46

603

30

64

30

60

Lanexa

649

649

60

49d

610

Toano

To Williamsburg

766

49c

Brickyard Landing

47

Chickahominy River

Little Creek Reservoir

623

49b

Morris Creek

5

Rustic

Gordon Island

49a

CHICKAHOMINY RIVERFRONT PARK

5

To 64

James River

The fishing: The largemouth-bass population in this lake is excellent. Lots of fish in the 14-to-19-inch range are taken every year. In addition, some larger specimens are caught.

Crappie up to 14 inches are common and pickerel and yellow perch numbers are good. Bluegill and redear up to 9 inches are abundant, while bowfin to 29 inches can be caught.

The best baits to use here are minnows, shad, night crawlers, corn (carp), and cut bait, plus spoons, plastic jigs, and crank baits.

Special regulations: No gasoline engines are allowed. Check bass regulations with the Virginia Department of Game and Inland Fisheries (VDGIF).

Access: There's a VDGIF ramp off Route 603.

Camping: Rock-a-Hock Campground, 1428 Outpost Road, Lanexa, VA 23089; (804) 966–2759; www.rockahock.com/welcome.htm.

For more information: VDGIF, 5806 Mooretown Rd., Williamsburg, VA 23188; (757) 253–4172; www.dgif.virginia.gov/fishing. Natural Resources Division, Public Utilities and Waterworks, City of Newport News, 2600 Washington Ave., Newport News, VA 23607; (757) 926–7177; www.newport-news.va.us/wwdept/welcome/history.htm.

47 Little Creek Reservoir (see map on page 82)

Key species: Largemouth and striped bass, crappie, yellow perch, pickerel.

Best time to fish: All year.

Directions: From Toano, take Route 610 (Forge Road) west to Route 766 (Lakeview Drive) south to the lake.

Description: This Newport News water-supply reservoir is relatively small. Large fluctuations in water levels are common. It is relatively deep and clear with little structure.

The fishing: Striped bass are stocked yearly. Fish over 20 pounds have been caught here. This species grows rapidly and everything indicates that this lake will remain a good striper fishery.

The largemouth-bass population in this lake is also good. Fish up to 11 pounds have been caught here. Pickerel to 19 inches and crappie to 14 inches are common. And this is one of the best lakes in Virginia in which to catch a citation yellow perch.

The best baits to use here are minnows, shad, night crawlers, jigs, swimming plugs, and crank baits.

Special regulations: No gasoline engines are allowed. No bank fishing. Open to fishing sunrise to sunset. Check regulations on species with the Virginia Department of Game and Inland Fisheries (VDGIF).

Striped bass over 20 pounds have been taken from Little Creek Reservoir.

Access: To reach the boat ramp from Toano, take Route 610 (Forge Road) west to Route 766 (Lakeview Drive) south to the lake. A 140-foot fishing pier and boat rentals are also available.

Camping: Rock-a-Hock Campground, 1428 Outpost Road, Lanexa, VA 23089; (804) 966–2759; www.rockahock.com/welcome.htm.

For more information: VDGIF, 5806 Mooretown Rd., Williamsburg, VA 23188; (757) 253–4172; www.dgif.virginia.gov/fishing/. Natural Resources Division, Public Utilities and Waterworks, City of Newport News, 2600 Washington Ave., Newport News, VA 23607; (757) 926–7177; www.newport-news.va.us/wwdept/welcome/history.htm. The lake concessionaire, (757) 566–1702; www.james-city.va.us.

48 The Lower James River

Key species: Largemouth bass, blue catfish, crappie, striped bass.

Best time to fish: March through October.

Directions: The Lower James runs through Richmond. Many bridges cross it within the city limits. Follow directions for individual accesses.

Description: The Lower James is defined as the section that runs from Richmond to the Chesapeake Bay. The fishing is very diversified. Many freshwater species and a large variety of saltwater fishes are available.

The fishing: Monster catfish are the signature of the James River. Blues up to 70 pounds have been caught and loads in the 30-to-60-pound range are taken every year. Anglers travel from around the country to get in on this fishery. Huge blues usually hang out around structures. Piers and trees next to deep water are good locations. Fresh bait is advantageous. Cast-net-caught threadfin shad or gizzard shad are excellent. Live white perch and eels also work. The best areas for blues are between Dutch Gap and Wards Creek and anywhere from Richmond to Hog Island. Fish at night in the summer, anytime the rest of the year.

The entire tidal James is home to channel cats, but the best flathead fishing is right in Richmond. Fish the pools between the fast water. In the spring and early summer, many flatheads are found upstream of Ancarrow's Landing in Richmond. Flathead catfish are primarily live-bait feeders. Almost any small fish will work.

The tidal James River has one the best largemouth-bass fisheries in the country. It has been the site of many high-stakes tournaments. Numerous trophies are caught in the area around Hopewell. Look for structure and old gravel pits. Do not overlook the larger tributaries.

The tributaries have the best fishing for crappie. Many 13-inch fish are caught. To find these guys, look for structure: submerged treetops and pier pilings.

Ocean-run rockfish are common in the James below Richmond, especially in the spring. It is particularly productive around the Interstate 95 bridge. During the fall season most of the fishing is found closer to the bay. The James River Bridge and the Monitor-Merrimac Bridge-Tunnel are hot spots.

White-perch angling is good throughout the river. Live minnows, grubs, beetle spins, or grass shrimp are best. Ten-pound-plus carp are common from Richmond downstream to Hog Island. Corn and dough are the baits of choice.

The best baits to use here, unless otherwise specified above, are live minnows, crawlers, cut bait, commercial catfish bait, minnow-imitating artificials, jigs, and plastics.

Fly patterns: Any pattern that looks like a minnow, shad, or herring.

Special regulations: For striped-bass regulations, contact the Virginia Marine Resources Commission (VMRC) in Newport News at (800) 541–4646.

Access: There are a number of Virginia Department of Game and Inland Fisheries (VDGIF) ramps, including the following:

Ancarrow's Landing in the city of Richmond on Maury Street (48a).

To find the Dutch Gap ramp, from Richmond take I–95 south to Route 10 east, turn north onto Route 732, then east onto Route 615 to the ramp (48b).

For the Osborne Pike Landing, take Route 5 southeast out of Richmond to Osborne Turnpike south (48c).

The Deep Bottom ramp is reached via Route 5 southeast out of Richmond.

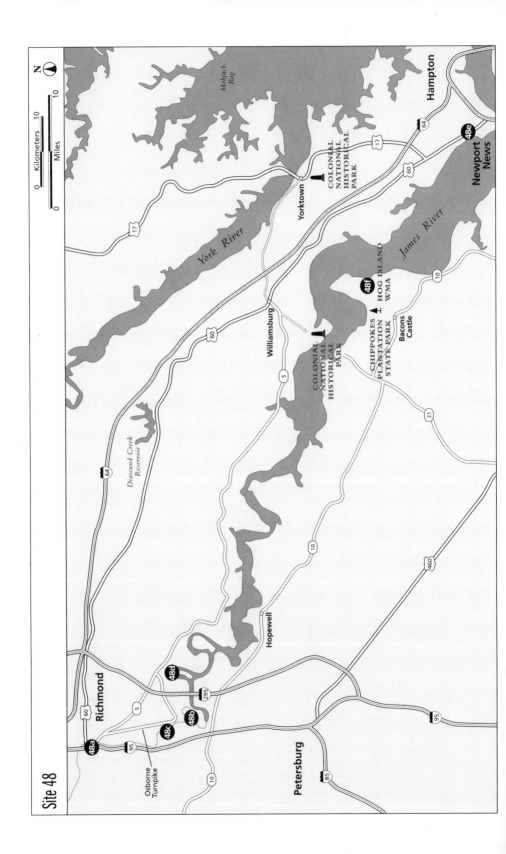

Site 48

N

0   Kilometers   10
0   Miles   10

Hampton

64

48e Newport News

17

60

Mobjack Bay

Yorktown

COLONIAL NATIONAL HISTORICAL PARK

17

York River

60

James River

10

48f HOG ISLAND WMA

Williamsburg

5

CHIPPOKES PLANTATION STATE PARK

Bacons Castle

COLONIAL NATIONAL HISTORICAL PARK

64

Diascund Creek Reservoir

31

Richmond

60

5

48d

295

48b

10

Hopewell

10

460

48a

95

48c

Osborne Turnpike

Petersburg

10

85

95

Turn south onto Kingsland Road, then go south onto Deep Bottom Road and follow it to Henrico County Park (48d).

Huntington Park in Newport News has a ramp. To reach it, follow Route 17 south out of Newport News to the foot of the James River Bridge (48e).

Another ramp is found at Lawnes Creek in the Hog Island Wildlife Management Area. From Bacons Castle, take Route 617 east to Route 650 north (48f).

For more information: VDGIF, 5806 Mooretown Rd., Williamsburg, VA 23188; (757) 253–4172; www.dgif.virginia.gov/fishing/. Anglers Cove Bait & Tackle, 9131 Staples Mill Road, Richmond, VA 23228; (804) 672-3474. Fin and Skin Taxidermy & Bait Shop, 2570 New Market Road, Richmond, VA 23231; (804) 795-5917.

Henrico County Park on the Lower James River is a great place to fish.

49 The Lower Chickahominy River and Lake (see map on page 82)

Key species: Largemouth bass, blue catfish, shad, herring, striped bass.

Best time to fish: All year.

Directions: From Richmond, take Route 60 east. Follow directions below to individual accesses.

Description: This river is a tributary of the Lower James River. The shoreline is lined with marshes and cypress trees. It's a very picturesque place to fish.

The fishing: Largemouth bass are the primary attraction in this river. The tidal Chickahominy is world-renowned for its bigmouths.

Blue catfish are the target of many anglers in the tidal Chickahominy. A good number of citation blues are caught every year. This is a great winter fishery.

Walkers Dam is the site of a big herring run each spring. It can get quite crowded at the peak of the season. Bare gold hooks, shad darts, small spinners, and spoons will all catch these silver bullets. Both hickory and white shad are also present, and striped bass will often follow the herring up river.

Spring is a nice time to fish the Chickahominy.

The best baits to use in this area, unless indicated otherwise above, are night crawlers, bloodworms, live minnows, prepared catfish bait, and cut bait. Crank baits, swimming plugs, jigs, spinners, shad darts, and plastics can also be used.

Special regulations: Check for special regulations on striped bass, shad, and herring with the Virginia Marine Resources Commission (VMRC), (800) 541–4646; www.mrc.state.va.us/regulations/regindex.shtm.

Access: To reach Chickahominy Riverfront Park from Williamsburg, take Route 5 west to the park (49a).

There's a primitive ramp at Chickahominy Wildlife Management Area. From Route 5 in Rustic, take Route 623 north to Morris Creek (49b).

From Route 60 in Toano, take Route 610 west to Brickyard Road (Route 618) south to reach the Brickyard Landing access point (49c).

Private (fee) ramps include Rock-a-Hock Campground (see below); Riverside Camp, (804) 966–5536; Colonial Harbor, (804) 966–5523; and River's Rest, (804) 829–2753. And Walkers Dam, accessed through Rock-a-Hock Campground, is located off Route 60 on Route 649, west of Lanexa (49d).

Camping: Rock-a-Hock Campground, 1428 Outpost Road, Lanexa, VA 23089; (804) 966–2759; www.rockahock.com/welcome.htm.

For more information: Chickahominy Riverfront Park, (757) 258–5020. Virginia Department of Game and Inland Fisheries (VDGIF), Chesapeake Office, 3909 Airline Blvd., Chesapeake, VA 23321; (757) 465–6811; www.dgif.virginia.gov/fishing/. Long Bay Pointe Bait and Tackle, 2109 W. Great Neck Rd., Virginia Beach, VA 23451; (757) 481–7517 (Captain Steve); www.longbaypointebaitandtackle.com.

50 Lakes Whitehurst and Smith

Key species: Walleye, largemouth bass, crappie, white perch, flathead catfish, sunfish.

Best time to fish: All year. Spring is best for walleye.

Directions: From Norfolk take Interstate 64 south to Route 13 east (Northampton Boulevard.) This crosses a culvert that connects the two lakes.

Description: These two lakes are separated by Northampton Boulevard (Route 13) in Virginia Beach. They are connected by a canal, but boats can not pass through.

The fishing: This is one of the best walleye fisheries in Virginia. The culvert under Northampton Boulevard is excellent for walleye in the early spring. Many Walleye up to 6 pounds are caught. Fishing for crappie and white perch is also good, with many over a pound. Plenty of largemouths over 14 inches and some larger than 20 inches can also be caught.

The best baits to use here are minnows, night crawler–spinner combos, spoons, jigs, and crank baits.

Special regulations: A Norfolk City Boating Permit is necessary in Whitehurst, and only engines 9.9 horsepower or smaller are allowed. Shore fishing is restricted to the piers.

Access: There's a dirt boat ramp on the Little Creek side on Northampton Boulevard, across the street from the Lake Smith Fishing Station. There are also two paved ramps in Whitehurst and two wheelchair-accessible fishing piers, plus a pier at Azalea Gardens.

For more information: Azalea Gardens, (757) 587–1755. Virginia Department of Game and Inland Fisheries (VDGIF), Chesapeake Office, 3909 Airline Blvd., Chesapeake, VA 23321; (757) 465–6811; www.dgif.virginia.gov/fishing/. Long Bay Pointe Bait and Tackle, 2109 W. Great Neck Rd., Virginia Beach, VA 23451; (757) 481–7517 (Captain Steve); www.longbaypointebaitandtackle.com.

51 Lake Airfield

Key species: Largemouth bass, crappie, sunfish, pickerel, yellow perch.

Best time to fish: December through April.

Directions: Take Route 628 south out of Wakefield to the lake.

Description: This 100-acre lake is surrounded by a very aesthetic native southeast Virginia forest. Lake Airfield straddles the Sussex and Southampton County border and is partially owned by the Virginia Department of Game and Inland Fisheries (VDGIF). It becomes rather clogged during the summer with abundant water lilies.

The fishing: Though the total biomass of fish in this lake is small, it produces some very nice-size specimens. Minnows and night crawlers are the best baits for this area. Plastics, surface and swimming lures, and flies are best for sunfish and bass.

Special regulations: Check the hours that fishing is allowed.

Access: There's a gravel VDGIF ramp. Follow the directions above.

For more information: VDGIF, 5806 Mooretown Rd., Williamsburg, VA 23188; (757) 253–4172; www.dgif.virginia.gov/fishing/. Long Bay Pointe Bait and Tackle, 2109 W. Great Neck Rd., Virginia Beach, VA 23451; (757) 481–7517 (Captain Steve); www.longbaypointebaitandtackle.com.

52 The Nottoway River

Key species: Large, smallmouth, and Roanoke bass, herring, sunfish, crappie, catfish, shad.

Best time to fish: All year.

Directions: From Norfolk take Interstate 64 south to Route 58 and go west. This crosses the Nottoway past the city of Franklin. Follow directions below to individual accesses.

Description: This southeast Virginia river gets it name from its origins in Nottoway County. Minimum development makes for a very scenic float. It begins near the Nottoway Court House and twists and turns for 130 miles before entering North Carolina below Franklin, Virginia.

The fishing: The upper Nottoway, above the Route 619 bridge on the Greensville–Sussex County line, is shallow with areas of rapids. Most anglers here fish for smallmouth and Roanoke bass and redbreast sunfish.

The lower Nottoway is slower and deeper. It is known for largemouths, channel cats, bluegill, redear, and crappie. Herring, shad, striped bass, and white perch are also available in the late winter and spring. Some trophy redears are caught here.

The best baits to use here are night crawlers, live minnows, and crickets. Crank baits, shad darts, swimming plugs, and plastics can also be used.

Access: Numerous access points are available for the Nottoway. Below find a list by county and route number. Some of the locations are labeled on the maps.

Lunenburg boat ramp: Route 49.

Dinwiddie: canoe accesses at Routes 613, 612, 610, and 609.

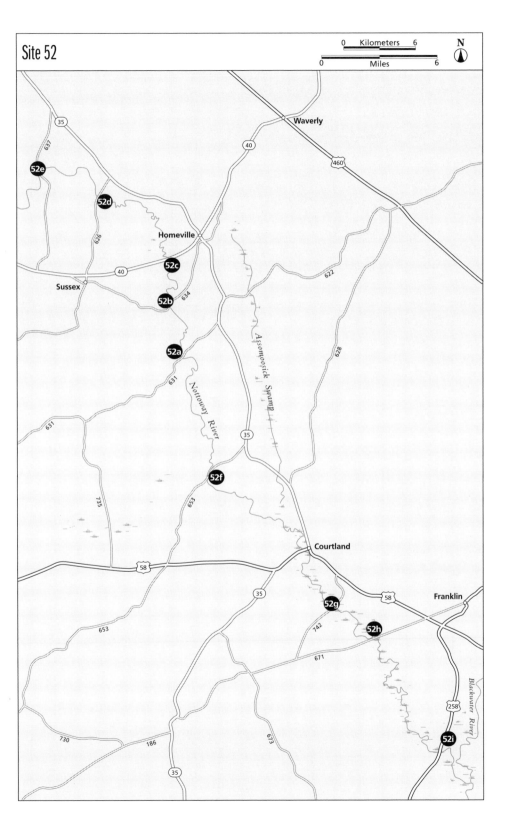

Site 52

Fishers put in for a day on the Nottoway River.

Sussex: boat ramps off Routes 619, 630, and 631 (52a). Canoe accesses at Routes 645, 40 (52c), 637 (52e), 626 (52d), and 634 (52b).

Southampton: boat ramps at Routes 653 (52f), 671 (52h), and 258 (52i). Canoe access at Route 742 (52g).

Besides these, a canoe or raft may be slipped into the river under one of the many bridges.

For more information: Virginia Department of Game and Inland Fisheries (VDGIF), Chesapeake Office, 3909 Airline Blvd., Chesapeake, VA 23321; (757) 465–6811; www.dgif.virginia.gov/fishing/. Long Bay Pointe Bait and Tackle, 2109 W. Great Neck Rd., Virginia Beach, VA 23451; (757) 481–7517 (Captain Steve); www.longbay pointebaitandtackle.com.

53 Western Branch Reservoir

Key species: Largemouth bass, crappie, redears, white and yellow perch.

Best time to fish: March through November.

Directions: From Norfolk take Route 58 west to Route 10 and go north. Follow directions below to individual accesses.

Description: Western Branch covers 1,265 acres and is a Norfolk water-supply lake. It is not very deep, at a maximum 35 feet. The lake is actually three lakes. Lake Prince is to the northwest and Lake Burnt Mills to the west with Western Branch in the middle. The three are separated by two dams.

The fishing: Many locals call this lake a fish factory. Striped bass are stocked every year and do well. Many good-size fish are caught. Most people troll lures like Rapalas or Rebels and also cast jigs. Live shad also work well. Fall and winter months are best. Try the spillways below the dams at Lakes Prince and Burnt Mills.

Bucket mouths do well in Western Branch with plenty of 12-to-16-inch fish available. A good number of trophies are caught every year.

This lake is known for panfishing and produces many trophy sunfish, white perch, yellow perch, and crappie. Shell-crackers are the primary target of many.

The best baits to use here are minnows, live shad, night crawlers, and cut bait. Spoons, jigs, trolling plugs, and crank baits can also be used.

Special regulations: City of Norfolk boating permits are required and may be purchased at the Norfolk Municipal Building, 400 Granby St., Norfolk (757) 664–6701, or at Lake Whitehurst. The maximum engine size is 9.9 horsepower. Bank fishing is prohibited.

Access: There's a Virginia Department of Game and Inland Fisheries (VDGIF) concrete ramp. To get there from Providence Church, follow Route 604 north to 605 east to the ramp.

There's also a ramp into Lake Prince. Rather than turning onto Route 605, continue on 604 to the ramp.

To reach the dirt ramp at Lake Burnt Mills Ramp, Continue on Route 604 to 603 east to the ramp.

For more information: VDGIF, Chesapeake Office, 3909 Airline Blvd., Chesapeake, VA 23321; (757) 465–6811; www.dgif.virginia.gov/fishing/. Long Bay Pointe Bait and Tackle, 2109 W. Great Neck Rd., Virginia Beach, VA 23451; (757) 481–7517 (Captain Steve); www.longbaypointebaitandtackle.com.

54 The North Landing River

Key species: Largemouth bass, bluegill, white catfish, striped bass, white perch.

Best time to fish: March through December.

Directions: The North Landing River runs through Virginia Beach. Take Salem Road south to the river and follow directions to individual accesses.

Description: This river is located in tidewater Virginia in the cities of Virginia Beach and Chesapeake. The North Landing is very slow moving so paddling against the current is possible. The water is brackish and salt- as well as freshwater species are present. It is a very nice place to fish by canoe.

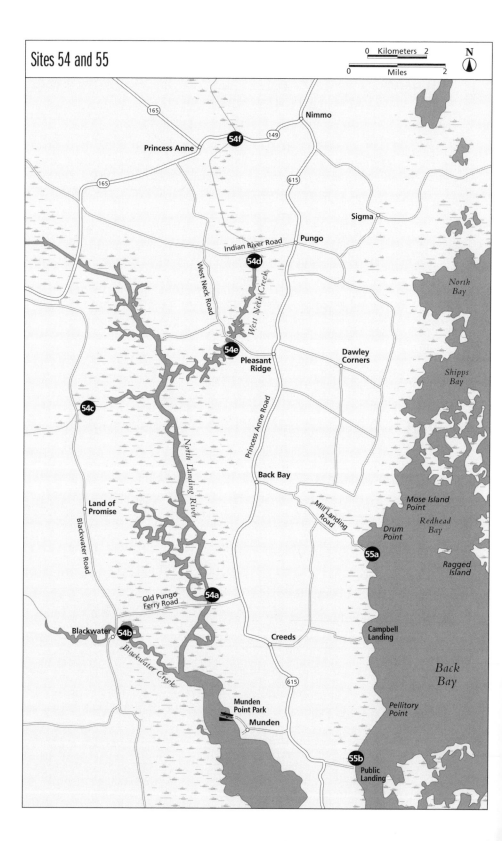

Sites 54 and 55

0 Kilometers 2
0 Miles 2

N

165

Nimmo

54f

149

Princess Anne

165

615

Sigma

Indian River Road   Pungo

West Neck Road

West Neck Creek

54d

North Bay

54e

Pleasant Ridge

Dawley Corners

Shipps Bay

54c

North Landing River

Princess Anne Road

Back Bay

Land of Promise

Blackwater Road

Mill Landing Road

Mose Island Point

Redhead Bay

Drum Point

55a

Ragged Island

Old Pungo Ferry Road

54a

Blackwater

54b

Blackwater Creek

Creeds

Campbell Landing

615

Back Bay

Munden Point Park

Munden

Pellitory Point

55b

Public Landing

The fishing: Fishing the North Landing can be divided into two parts. The main stem of the river holds more of the brackish and saltwater species while freshwater fish dominate in the tributaries. White perch and white catfish, along with stripers, are primarily found in the main stem. Tributaries like the Pocaty and West Neck Creek hold sunfish and bass.

The best baits to use here are night crawlers, bloodworms, live minnows, and cut bait. Crank baits, swimming plugs, jigs, and plastics can also be used.

Special regulations: Check special regulations on striped bass. Contact the Virginia Marine Resources Commission (VMRC) in Newport News at (800) 541–4646.

Access points: Some of the following are noted on the map. Boat ramps are available at Virginia Beach.

Pungo Ferry Marina (54a), 2272 Old Pungo Ferry Rd.; (757) 721–6569.

West Neck Marina (54e), 3985 West Neck Rd.

Blackwater Trading Post (54b), 5605 Blackwater Rd.; (757) 421–2803.

Munden Point Park, 2001 Pefley Lane. Take Munden Point Road east from Route 615 to Pefly Lane. Follow it to the park.

Launch sites for canoes and car-topper boats include Dozier's Bridge (54f), spanning West Neck Creek at 2500 block of Route 149 (Princess Anne Road), and Speed's Bridge (54d) at West Neck Creek at the 2200 block of Indian River Road. Limited parking is available at both areas.

Another launch site is the Pocaty Creek Bridge (54c) at the 400 block of Blackwater Road. Parking here is also limited. And there's the North Landing River Nature Preserve at the 4800 block of Blackwater Road. Canoes must be carried about ½ mile to the water.

For more information: Virginia Department of Game and Inland Fisheries (VDGIF), Chesapeake Office, 3909 Airline Blvd., Chesapeake, VA 23321; (757) 465–6811; www.dgif.virginia.gov/fishing/. Long Bay Pointe Bait and Tackle, 2109 W. Great Neck Rd., Virginia Beach, VA 23451; (757) 481–7517 (Captain Steve); www.longbaypointebaitandtackle.com.

55 Back Bay *(see map on page 94)*

Key species: Salt water: Flounder, sea trout, spot, croakers. *Freshwater:* Largemouth bass, crappie, white perch, channel catfish.

Best time to fish: March through November.

Directions: Back Bay is in the extreme southeast corner of Virginia Beach. Take Route 165 south from Virginia Beach to West Neck Road. Go south to Indian River Road and head east. In Pungo, turn south onto Princess Anne Road, then east onto Muddy Creek Road. Follow directions to individual accesses.

Description: Covering 25,000 acres, Back Bay is the largest body of water in the district. The main body is brackish with many feeder streams and creeks that are fresh.

The fishing: This restricted body of water has a diverse fishery. The brackish water contains salty species and the freshwater tributaries contain bass, crappie, cats, and sunfish.

In the past this area has produced many citation largemouths, but an as yet undetermined problem occurred a number of years ago and now they are more difficult to come by. It is expected that the fish will come back over time. The area still produces many large channel cats and white perch.

The best baits to use here are minnows, night crawlers, sea worms, clams, and cut bait. Spoons, jigs, and crank baits can also be used.

Bank fishing is restricted to a few of the tributaries and the boat ramp areas.

Special regulations: For saltwater species regulations, contact the Virginia Marine Resources Commission (VMRC) in Newport News at (800) 541–4646.

Access: Take Route 615 (Princess Anne Road) south to Back Bay, then head east on Mill Landing Road (622) to a ramp (55a). You can also take Princess Anne Road south to Public Landing Road east to another ramp (55b).

For more information: Virginia Department of Game and Inland Fisheries (VDGIF), Chesapeake Office, 3909 Airline Blvd., Chesapeake, VA 23321; (757) 465–6811; www.dgif.virginia.gov/fishing/. Long Bay Pointe Bait and Tackle, 2109 W. Great Neck Rd., Virginia Beach, VA 23451; (757) 481–7517 (Captain Steve); www.longbaypointebaitandtackle.com.

South-central Virginia

South-central Virginia is big bass country. Along with giant largemouths and super-slab-size crappie, stocked striped bass are also featured.

56 The Upper James River

Key species: Catfish, musky, small, bigmouth, and spotted bass.

Best time to fish: February through November.

Directions: The Upper James River runs through a large swath of central Virginia. From Richmond take Route 6 west. Almost every crossroad running north/south will lead to or cross the river. Follow directions to individual accesses.

Description: This river flows through southwestern Virginia in addition to the south-central region. The Upper James begins in Alleghany County where the Cowpasture and Jackson Rivers come together near the city of Clifton Forge. It runs through the mountains to Lynchburg. The river then enters the piedmont and flows to Richmond. Below the state capital we define the river as the Lower James. This river is best fished from a canoe, but small boats may also be launched. In addition, plenty of bank access is available.

The fishing: Both the mountain and piedmont sections of the Upper James offer great fishing for smallmouths as well as rock bass. Anglers also have a good chance to hook into a musky. Both flathead and channel catfish are available throughout most of the river, as are redears. Some sections hold large gar, which can add some excitement. Bank fishing from the many access points is possible. Some may prefer float trips.

The best baits to use here are night crawlers, crawdads, and live minnows or leeches. Minnow-imitating artificials and plastics can also be used.

Fly patterns: Any pattern that looks like a minnow, crawfish, or leech.

Access points: Here are just a few of the many access points.

Unless otherwise noted, these all have good ramps: Horseshoe Bend off Route 43 (56a); a canoe launch under Route 630 bridge in Springwood; off Route 11 in Buchanan (56b); a canoe launch under the Route 614 bridge in Arcadia (56c); a canoe launch near Glasgow off Route 501 (56d); at the end of Route 652 in Elon; on Route 56 in Wingina (56e); the James River Wildlife Management Area on Route 626 (56f); in Howardsville off Route 602 (56g); in Scottsville downstream of the Route 20 bridge (56h); and the Hardware River Wildlife Management Area located west of Central Plains. Take Route 6 to Route 640 south. Follow to the WMA (56i).

Site 56

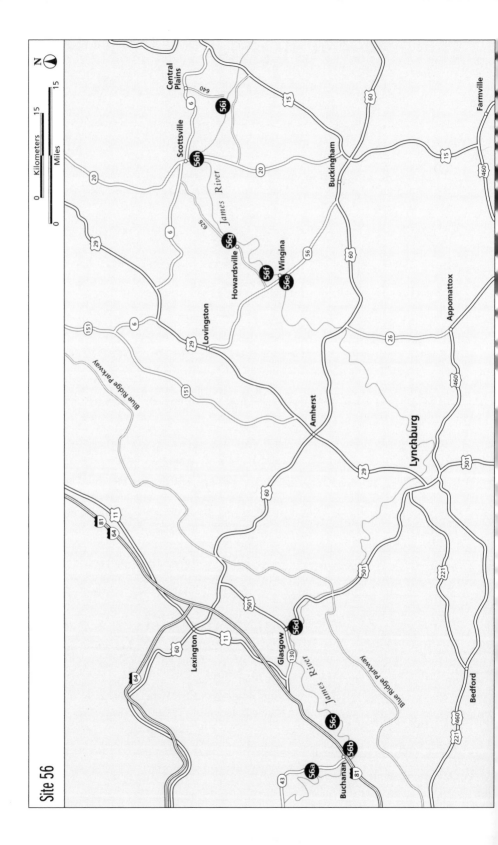

There's a dam below Snowden, but do not attempt to drift this area. Class II and III rapids are present below this area through the James River Gorge. Only experienced drifters should attempt this part of the river.

Camping: George Washington National Forest, 810-A Madison Ave., Covington, VA 24426; (540) 962–2214; www.fs.fed.us/r8/gwj/jamesriver/. James River State Park, Route 1, Box 787, Gladstone, VA 24553; (434) 933–4355; www.state.va.us/dcr/parks/jamesriv.htm.

This Web site describes a number of float trips on the Upper James: www.dgif .virginia.gov/fishing/waterbodies/display.asp?id=158&section=maps.

For more information: Virginia Department of Game and Inland Fisheries (VDGIF), 1132 Thomas Jefferson Rd., Forest, VA 24551-9223; (434) 525–7522; www.dgif.virginia.gov/fishing/.

57 Bear Creek Lake

Key species: Largemouth bass, panfish, catfish.

Best time to fish: March through October.

Directions: From Farmville, take Route 45 north to Route 60 west. Turn north onto Route 629 (Oak Hill Road) to Bear Creek Lake State Park. You will pass close to boat ramps at Winston Lake and Arrowhead Lake. You may want to try those also.

Description: Bear Creek Lake is a small pond of about 40 acres. It was reclaimed by the Virginia Department of Game and Inland Fisheries (VDGIF) in the 1990s and supports some fine fishing.

The fishing: This lake supports a large population of largemouths. Crappie and bluegills are also abundant and those wanting channel cats will not be disappointed.

The best baits to use here are night crawlers, crawfish, live minnows, lures that imitate minnows, spinner baits, jigs, plastics, and surface lures.

Fly patterns: Muddlers, crawfish patterns, and deer-hair bugs. Poppers also work.

Access: The park has a concrete boat ramp and maintains a wheelchair-accessible fishing pier. Boat rentals are available.

Camping: Bear Creek Lake State Park, 929 Oak Hill Rd., Cumberland, VA 23040; (804) 492–4410; www.dcr.state.va.us/parks/bearcreek.htm.

For more information: VDGIF, 1700 S. Main St., Farmville, VA 23901; (434) 392–9645; www.dgif.virginia.gov/fishing/.

58 Holliday Lake

Key species: Largemouth bass, pickerel, yellow perch, crappie.

Best time to fish: All year but best in late winter and early spring.

Nice bass can be caught at Holliday Lake.

Directions: Take Route 24 northeast from Appomattox, turn east onto Route 626, then north onto 640 and east onto 692.

Description: Holliday Lake is in the state park that bears its name. Its clear waters cover 145 acres and it's a great place to have a family outing.

The fishing: Bigmouths are the favorite of most who fish Holliday. They run all sizes from 4 inches to over 20. Numerous sunken trees offer cover for these guys, but fish deep in the summer.

While a few bluegill are present, yellow perch dominate the lake. Crappie and channel cats are also available.

The best baits to use here are minnows, jigs, and plastics.

Fly patterns: Deer-hair bugs, poppers.

Special regulations: Check with Virginia Department of Game and Inland Fisheries (VDGIF) for special regulations on bass.

Access: A paved ramp is available.

Camping and accommodations: The state park has campsites available as well as the accommodations described here.

Appomattox Victorian Rental, P.O. Box 1058, Appomattox, VA 24522; (434) 352–8539; www.appomattoxvictorianrental.com.

Longacre B&B, 1670 Church Street, Appomattox, VA 24522; (434) 352–9251 or (800) 758–7730; www.longacreva.com.

Spring Grove Farm Bed & Breakfast, Route 4, Box 259, Appomattox, VA 24522; (434) 352–7429; www.springgrovefarm.com.

For more information: Holliday Lake State Park, (434) 248–6308 (park office) or (800) 933–PARK (reservations); www.dcr.state.va.us/parks/holliday.htm. VDGIF, 1700 S. Main St., Farmville, VA 23901; (434) 392–9645; www.dgif.virginia.gov/fishing/.

59 The Appomattox River

Key species: Kentucky spotted, smallmouth, and largemouth bass, pickerel, sunfish species. Stripers and walleyes are seasonal.

Best time to fish: March through November.

Directions: This river's headwaters are in Appomattox County. It flows by Farmville and forms the boundaries between a bunch of central Virginia counties, namely Buckingham, Prince Edward, Cumberland, Amelia, Powhatan, Chesterfield, Dinwiddie, and Prince George.

Description: This is a long river and is a major tributary of the James River.

The fishing: The Appomattox has a good population of Kentucky spotted bass. They were introduced and have become quite successful. If you would like to catch one of these fighters, fish from upstream of Farmville down to the Amelia-Chesterfield county line at Route 360 west of Richmond.

Large and smallmouth bass in addition to redbreast sunfish, bluegill, crappie, pickerel, and chubs are abundant. Striped bass and walleye run out of Lake Chesdin and can be caught in the spring.

The best baits to use here are night crawlers, crawdads, live minnows or leeches, and plastics. Deep-diving crank baits work well in deeper sections.

Access: Access is limited to bridge crossings.

Camping and accommodations: Holliday Lake State Park, Route 2, Box 622, Appomattox, VA 24522; (434) 248–6308; www.state.va.us/dcr/parks/holliday.htm. Long Wood Inn, 408 High St., Farmville, VA 23901; (434) 392–1773; www.longwood inn.com.

For more information: Virginia Department of Game and Inland Fisheries (VDGIF), 1700 S. Main St., Farmville, VA 23901; (434) 392–9645; www.dgif .virginia.gov/fishing/.

Pocahontas State Park offers great shore fishing opportunities.

60 Pocahontas State Park: Swift Creek Lake and Beaver Lake

Key species: Largemouth bass, sunfish species, carp, pickerel, catfish.

Best time to fish: March through November.

Directions: From Richmond, take Interstate 95 south. At exit 61 go west on Route 10 to Route 655 (Beach Road). The park is 4 miles farther on the right.

Description: Both lakes are within the Pocahontas State Park. Boating on Swift Creek Lake, which comprises 107 acres, is restricted to self-powered or electric motors. No private boats are allowed on Beaver Lake. Canoes, paddleboats, and rowboats may be rented.

The fishing: These lakes support populations of largemouths, bluegills, redears, carp, and pickerel. Catfish are also available.

The best baits to use here are night crawlers, live minnows, lures that imitate minnows, spinner baits, jigs, plastics, and surface lures.

Access: Boat rentals are available.

Camping and accommodations: Pocahontas State Park, 10301 State Park Rd., Chesterfield, VA 23832-6355; (804) 796–4255 or (800) 933–PARK; www.dcr.state.va.us/parks/pocahont.htm.

The park also has a number of cabins for rent.

For more information: Virginia Department of Game and Inland Fisheries (VDGIF), 4010 W. Broad St., Richmond, VA 23230; (804) 367–1000; www.dgif .virginia.gov/fishing/.

61 Lake Chesdin

Key species: Largemouth bass, bluegill, channel catfish, white perch, walleye.

Best time to fish: March through January, but good fishing can also be had all winter long.

Directions: Follow directions to individual accesses.

Description: Lake Chesdin, aka Chesdin Reservoir, is a large impoundment of over 3,000 acres. It is conveniently located within reasonable driving distances of Richmond, Hampton Roads, and Washington, D.C.

The fishing: Very good angling for largemouth bass and crappie is to be had in Lake Chesdin. There is quite a bit of pressure so it takes time to catch nicer-size fish.

Chesdin is not known for its striped-bass fishery. However, some line-siders are available in the lake and some nice-size fish are taken every year.

Fine walleye are produced in Chesdin. The stocking of this species has been increased in recent years, so this excellent fishery should continue.

Bluegill numbers have decreased in recent years. Some fishery biologists believe this is because of the large increase in white perch. These silver beauties are excellent to eat and are found all over the lake. They take worms, minnows, small jigs, and other lures.

The catfish fishery is underutilized in Chesdin. A number of different species are present, but channel cats predominate.

Access: To reach a concrete boat ramp from Petersburg, take Route 460 west, go north on Route 632 (Olgers Road), west on Route 601 (River Road), and north on Route 776 (Chesdin Lake Road). A fishing pier is also located here.

There's public access to shore fishing alongside the bridges off Route 623 (Sutherland Road).

Camping and Marinas: Whippernock Marina, 2700 Sutherland Rd., Sutherland, VA 23885; (804) 265–5252. Cozy Cove Campground, 713 Sutherland Rd., Church Road, VA 23833; (804) 265–9000.

For more information: Virginia Department of Game and Inland Fisheries (VDGIF), 4010 W. Broad St., Richmond, VA 23230; (804) 367–1000; www.dgif.virginia.gov/ fishing/. Chesterfield County Chamber of Commerce, 9330-B Iron Bridge Rd., Chesterfield, VA 23832; (804) 748–6364; www.chesterfieldchamber.com.

A beautiful sunrise promises a fine day of fishing at Briery Creek Lake. The pier is in the background.

62 Briery Creek Lake

Key species: Largemouth bass, crappie, bluegill, redear sunfish.

Best time to fish: March through November, but the best fishing is just as water temperatures reach 60 degrees F.

Directions: From Farmville, take Route 15 south. Turn west at Route 790 to access the dam area or continue on 15 and turn west onto Route 701.

Description: Briery Creek Lake is owned by the Virginia Department of Game and Inland Fisheries (VDGIF) and covers over 800 acres. Timber was left standing when the dam was completed. This left an excess of great cover for largemouth bass. It is known as Virginia's largemouth bass trophy experiment.

The fishing: Briery was conceived as a trophy bass lake, and it is a success. Most anglers in Briery are trying to get that 10-pound-plus lunker bucket mouth. This lake is probably the best fishery for trophy largemouths in the state. The initial stocking was with both the Florida and northern strains of this species. It has been very successful. The best time to catch a lunker is just as the water temperature reaches 60 degrees F in the spring. This is the time that the fish come into the shallows to spawn.

Most fishers use large minnows or jigs. Many fish off the dam and plenty of shore-line is accessible.

Very large crappie are also taken here. Winter is best and many fish after dark off the shore or pier. Be careful where you step at night during warm weather, as snakes are abundant.

The best baits to use here are minnows, jigs, large swimming and surface plugs, and plastics.

Fly patterns: Deer-hair bugs, poppers.

Special regulations: Check with the VDGIF (see below) for special regulations on bass. Boating is restricted to daylight.

Access: There are boat ramps at the dam off Route 790 and at the end of Route 701. A covered, wheelchair-accessible fishing pier is located off Route 790.

Accommodations: Long Wood Inn, 408 High St., Farmville, VA 23901; (434) 392–1773; www.longwoodinn.com.

For more information: VDGIF, 1700 S. Main St., Farmville, VA 23901; (434) 392–9645; www.dgif.virginia.gov/fishing/. Farmville Chamber of Commerce, 116 North Main St., Farmville, VA 23901; (434) 392–3939; http://chamber.farmville.net.

63 Sandy River Reservoir

Key species: Largemouth bass, pickerel, crappie, bluegill.

Best time to fish: March through November.

Directions: From Farmville, go east on Route 460 and turn south on Route 640. The first left (east) leads to the boat ramp.

Description: This 740-acre reservoir was built by Prince Edward County in 1994. It was opened to fishing in 1996.

The fishing: The largemouth-bass fishery in this lake is excellent. Numerous fish in the 6-to-10-pound range are caught. The best fishing is in the spring, but summer angling is good at night or early morning.

Crappie are also abundant, especially in winter. Bluegill provide plenty of action at times. Channel cats are stocked and some good-size specimens are consistently taken.

The best baits to use here are minnows, jigs, large swimming and surface plugs, and plastics.

Fly patterns: Deer-hair bugs, poppers.

Special regulations: Check with the Virginia Department of Game and Inland Fisheries (VDGIF) for special regulations on this lake. Outboard motors under 10 horsepower are allowed.

The pier at Sandy River Reservoir offers beautiful scenery and good fishing.

Access: Both a boat ramp and fishing pier are located on this lake. Follow directions above.

Accommodations: Long Wood Inn, 408 High St., Farmville, VA 23901; (434) 392–1773; www.longwoodinn.com.

For more information: VDGIF, 1700 S. Main St., Farmville, VA 23901; (434) 392–9645; www.dgif.virginia.gov/fishing/. Farmville Chamber of Commerce, 116 North Main St., Farmville, VA 23901; (434) 392–3939; www.chamber.farmville.net.

64 The Meherrin River

Key species: Largemouth and rock bass, channel catfish, bluegill, crappie, shad.

Best time to fish: February through November.

Directions: From Richmond take Interstate 95 south. The river crosses I-95 at Emporia. Follow directions below to individual accesses.

Description: The Meherrin flows through agricultural as well as forest lands before emptying into the Emporia Reservoir. Its waters flow over the Emporia Dam and continue on into North Carolina. Below the dam, caution is advised for wading or bank-fishing anglers as the water levels fluctuate greatly. It is quite swampy below the dam.

The fishing: Most Meherrin anglers use bait. Crickets and worms for panfish and catties and minnows for bass are the most popular. Some who want to fish exclusively for bass cast small jigs or crank baits. There's a good shad run in the spring. Cast darts below the dam.

The best baits to use overall are night crawlers; crawdads; live minnows, crickets, or leeches; crank baits; and plastics.

Access: Access to the Meherrin is limited. Most of the ramps are in Emporia Reservoir with one below the dam. However, fishing and canoe access is possible at many of the bridges that cross the river.

There's access above the dam in Emporia. When Route 58W passes over I–95, turn south on Wiggins and follow it to the end to reach it. Below the dam there's a wheelchair-accessible concrete ramp at Meherrin Park. Off Route 301, travel east on Hicksford Avenue onto Meherrin Park Road.

For more information: VDGIF, Chesapeake Office, 3909 Airline Blvd., Chesapeake, VA 23321; (757) 465–6811; www.dgif.virginia.gov/fishing/. Emporia-Greensville Chamber of Commerce, 400 Halifax St., Emporia, VA 23847; (434) 634–9441; www.emporia-greensvillechamber.com.

65 Brunswick County Lake

Key species: Largemouth bass, crappie, sunfish, yellow perch.

Best time to fish: All year.

Directions: From Edgerton, take Route 58 east to Route 638 north (County Pound Road) to the lake.

Description: This 150-acre lake is owned by the Virginia Department of Game and Inland Fisheries (VDGIF), and the entire shoreline is open to the public.

The fishing: Many come to Brunswick for the large yellow perch, but very nice shell-crackers and bluegill are abundant. Crappie fishing is also good, with some up to 14 inches. Plenty of largemouths over 14 inches and some larger than 20 inches are also available.

The best baits to use here are minnows, night crawlers, plastics, jigs, and surface and swimming lures.

Fly patterns: Bream busters and tiny poppers.

Access: A boat ramp and fishing pier are available. Follow directions above.

For more information: VDGIF, 1320 Belman Rd., Fredericksburg, VA 22401; (540) 899–4169; www.dgif.virginia.gov/fishing/.

Many come to Brunswick County Lake to fish for large yellow perch.

66 Great Creek Watershed Lake

Key species: Largemouth bass, crappie, channel cats, sunfish.

Best time to fish: March through November.

Directions: The lake is off Route 46, approximately 1 mile north of the town of Lawrenceville. Look for the junior high school.

Description: This 200-acre lake is in Brunswick County. It is a very pleasant place to spend a day fishing with kids.

The fishing: Great Creek has a good largemouth-bass population. Crappie and sunfish are also abundant, and channel catfish are stocked yearly.

Special regulations: Be sure to check bass regulations and legal hours. No gasoline engines.

Access: A boat ramp and pier are available.

For more information: VDGIF, 1320 Belman Rd., Fredericksburg, VA 22401; (540) 899–4169; www.dgif.virginia.gov/fishing/. Brunswick County Administrator's office: (804) 848–3107.

67 Lake Gordon

Key species: Channel cats, largemouth bass, crappie, redears.

Best time to fish: March through November.

Directions: From South Hill, take Route 1 south (Route 58 west) to Route 664. Turn right (west) on Route 799 to the lake.

Description: This lake is owned by the Virginia Department of Game and Inland Fisheries (VDGIF) and covers about 150 acres. Motors under 10 horsepower are allowed.

The fishing: Gordon has a fine population of channel catfish. Use commercial catfish baits or cut herring. Nice bass, some over 20 inches, are also found here. Crappie and redear populations are also reasonable.

The best baits to use here are jigs, plastics, surface lures, night crawlers, commercial catfish bait, and live minnows.

Fly patterns: Bass bugs, poppers, mosquito and bream busters.

Access: This area has a paved boat ramp.

For more information: VDGIF, 1132 Thomas Jefferson Rd., Forest, VA 24551-9223; (434) 525–7522; www.dgif.virginia.gov/fishing/.

68 The Dan River

Key species: Upstream: Trout. *Downstream:* Largemouth, striped, and white bass, catfish, white perch.

Best time to fish: All year.

Directions: To get to the upper portion of the river, take Route 58 west from Stuart to Route 610 north (Cloudbreak Road) just before Vesta. This road changes names a few times but remains 610. It follows the Dan for quite a distance. Alternatively, take Route 58 east from the town Meadows of Dan to Route 632 south. This road follows the river.

The lower river passes through Danville and South Boston.

Description: Though the Dan flows in both the southwestern and south-central regions as described in this book, we place it in the South-central region.

From high in the Blue Ridge in Patrick County to the John H. Kerr Reservoir near Clarksville, the Dan River is a stream of contrasts. From a bubbling fast native trout stream at higher altitudes, it evolves into a slow meandering river where it empties into the reservoir.

The fishing: The upper Dan has excellent trout angling. Once the river flows into North Carolina past the Route 103 bridge, trout peter out. When it passes back into

Virginia a few miles west of Danville, it emerges as a sunfish, largemouth-bass, and catfish stream.

Striped-bass fishing in the Dan usually starts in late April. It occurs downstream of Danville. Flathead and blue-cat fishing is excellent in the lower Dan. A good run of walleye is also available during the winter and white perch and white bass in the spring.

The best baits to use here are night crawlers, crawdads, live minnows, cut bait, and leeches; also flies for trout, jigs and spoons for stripers and perch, and plastics for bass.

Special regulations: The upper Dan has a number of trout-fishing areas with varying regulations. Please check before wetting your line. Virginia and North Carolina have a reciprocal license agreement for some of the sections that run through both states. Be sure to check the regulation books of both states. In certain areas a free permit is required from the City of Danville. See contact info below.

Special regulations also apply on stripers, bass, catfish, walleye, and others. Check the regulations.

Access: There's a canoe launch at Talbott Dam off Route 601. Anglers can also hike below the dam. Another canoe launch is located at Townes Reservoir off Route 602. In Dan River Park in Danville, there's a ramp on the south side of the river located just upstream from the Route 51 bridge off Route 29.

On Route 58 east out of Danville, keep an eye out for River Point Road. This is at Anglers' Park. There's lots of opportunities for bank fishing here along walking and bike trails.

From Route 58, take Routes 304/360 and follow the signs to the Virginia Department of Game and Inland Fisheries (VDGIF) boat landing in South Boston.

The VDGIF ramp off Route 58 is 12 miles downstream from South Boston at the mouth of the Hyco River.

Two ramps are accessible from Route 344 at Staunton River State Park.

Also see the Trout Fishing chapter for upstream areas.

Camping: Staunton River State Park, 1170 Staunton Trail, Scottsburg, VA 24589-9636; (434) 572–4623; www.state.va.us/dcr/parks/staunton.htm.

For more information: VDGIF, 1132 Thomas Jefferson Rd., Forest, VA 24551-9223; (434) 525–7522; www.dgif.virginia.gov/fishing/. City of Danville, Director of Electric Division, Department of Utilities, P.O. Box 33007, Danville, VA 24543; (434) 799–5270; www.danville-va.gov/.

Blue catfish up to 90 pounds can be caught at Kerr Dam below Buggs Island Lake.

69 Buggs Island Lake (Kerr Reservoir)

Key species: Crappie, largemouth bass, striped bass, white bass, catfish.

Best time to fish: March through January, but good fishing can also be had all winter long.

Directions: From Richmond, head south on Interstate 95. Turn west onto Route 460, then south on Interstate 85. At South Hill turn west onto Route 58. This will bring you to the general area.

Description: Buggs Island is a large lake, almost 50,000 acres. It is located on the Virginia–North Carolina border, but Virginia fishing licenses are valid throughout the lake. Facilities are plentiful in the area.

The fishing: Crappie are plentiful and large in Buggs Island. It is one the best places in Virginia to fish for these small scrappers. Late winter and early spring are the best times to fish for these guys, but they are caught all year. Grassy, Butcher, and Bluestone Creeks are very productive.

Two-to-four-pound largemouths are common. Anglers are encouraged to fish cover but the location of such is very dependent on water level. Many consider this body of water among the best bass waters in the country.

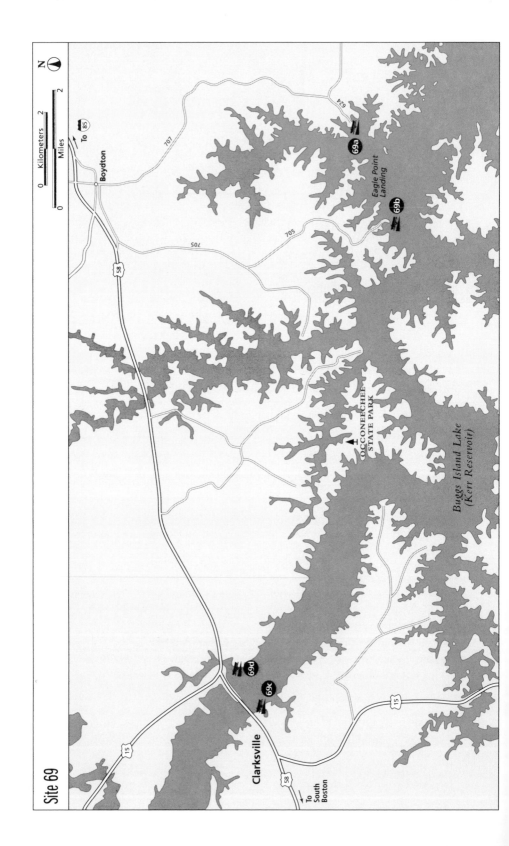

Site 69

Striped-bass angling is also good. Fishers are encouraged to keep any legal fish during the summer months because many die if released into warm water.

Good populations of blue, channel, and flathead catfish are also present.

The best baits to use here are live minnows, night crawlers, spinner baits, and plastics.

Fly patterns: for striped bass, Black Phantom and any shad pattern.

Access: The Virginia Department of Game and Inland Fisheries (VDGIF) maintains a boat ramp at Hyco River Route 58. It's at the western end of the lake near South Boston. There are also ramps on Route 4 north of Palmer Point Road; off of Route 635; on Route 624/Eastland Creek Road (69a); at the end of Route 705 (69b); off Route 58 in Clarksville (69c); and on Route 15, below the north end of the bridge (69d).

The state parks have ramps, and private facilities are also available.

Camping: Occoneechee State Park, (434) 374–2210; www.dcr.state.va.us/parks. From I–85, take the Route 58 west exit at South Hill. The park is located on Route 58, 1 mile east of Clarksville

Staunton River State Park (800–933–PARK; www.state.va.us/dcr/parks/staunton.htm) is located 18 miles east of South Boston. Take Route 360 to Route 344. Follow Route 344 for 10 miles to the park, located southeast of Scottsburg.

For more information: Contact the U.S. Army Corps of Engineers at (804) 738–6371 for current lake water-level information. A current fishing report is available at www.kerrlake.info/fishing/index.htm. Clarksville Lake Chamber of Commerce, 105 Second Street, P.O. Box 1017, Clarksville, VA 23927-1017; (434) 374–2436 or (800) 557–5582; www.clarksvilleva.com.

70 Lake Gaston

Key species: Crappie, largemouth bass, striped bass, white bass, catfish.

Best time to fish: March through January, but good fishing can also be had all winter long, especially for walleye.

Directions: From Richmond, head south on Interstate 95. Near Emporia, turn west onto Route 611, then south on Route 46. To get to the Virginia portion of the lake, take Route 665 southwest through Gasburg, then Route 666. This will bring you to the general area. Or from South Hill, take Route 1 south.

Description: Gaston is a large lake—over 20,000 acres. Most of it is in North Carolina, but Virginia licenses are valid throughout the lake.

The fishing: Gaston has excellent largemouth fishing. Two-to-four-pound largemouths are common. Weed beds and cover are the preferred locations.

Striped bass have been stocked by the North Carolina DNR. The fast water below Kerr Dam is excellent for line-siders. Fishers are encouraged to keep any legal fish during the summer months because many die if released into warm water.

Good populations of blue, channel, and flathead catfish are also present. The Virginia state record for blue cats was caught here. There's also excellent fishing for cats and stripers in spring in the race under Kerr Dam.

The best baits to use are live minnows, night crawlers, spinner baits, and plastics.

Fly patterns: For striped bass, Black Phantom and any shad pattern.

Access: Take Interstate 85 in North Carolina to Route 1 north, then head west on Route 61, south on Route 616, and northwest on Route 4. Take this over the dam, turn right, and follow it down to the river.

All of the Virginia Department of Game and Inland Fisheries (VDGIF) boat ramps are wheelchair-accessible. Here are just a few of the many access points:

Head east on Route 626 from Gasburg and turn north on Route 705 to reach the Pea Hill access point.

Take Route 58 west from Brodnax and turn south on Route 626 to reach Poplar Creek.

From South Hill, take Route 1 southwest to Steel Bridge.

From Route 1 south, take Route 711 west to Route 710 west to Route 4 north. Go over the Kerr Dam and turn right (north).

Camping: Americamps Lake Gaston, (434) 636–2668; www.americampslake gaston.com.

For more information: Lake Gaston Chamber of Commerce, 2475 Eaton Ferry Rd., Littleton, NC 27850; (866) 730–5711 or (252) 586–5711; www.lakegaston chamber.com. VDGIF, 1320 Belman Rd., Fredericksburg, VA 22401; (540) 899–4169; www.dgif.virginia.gov/fishing/.

Southwestern Virginia

Southwestern Virginia, like the central area of the state, has great largemouth fishing. However, along with the buckets, fantastic smallmouth and trout angling is also available.

71 The Jackson River

Key species: Upstream: Smallmouth and rock bass and rainbow and brown trout. *Downstream:* Smallmouth and rock bass.

Best time to fish: All year.

Directions: Above Lake Moomaw, Route 603 parallels the Jackson River for a distance. Private land is abundant here so be sure that you are always on Forest Service property.

Below Moomaw, bridge crossings on Routes 638, 641, 687, and others provide access to the river. The Jackson then flows through Covington and then along Route 60 to Clifton Forge.

Description: The Jackson flows both above and below Lake Moomaw. Fast water abounds in the upper river while it meanders further downstream.

The fishing: Above Lake Moomaw the Jackson provides excellent smallmouth-bass, rainbow-trout, and brown-trout fishing. Large lake-run rainbows and browns are available in the autumn in this section. Between Gathright Dam and Covington, rainbow and brown trout abound as well as smallmouth and rock bass and redbreast sunfish. Downstream of Covington, trout peter out, but anglers will find numerous opportunities for smallmouth bass, redbreast sunfish, and rock bass.

The best baits to use here are night crawlers, crawdads, live minnows, cut bait, and leeches. Use flies for trout.

Special regulations: Check trout fishing regulations with the Virginia Department of Game and Inland Fisheries (VDGIF).

Access: Numerous access points will be found between Covington and Clifton Forge.

Camping: The U.S. Forest Service runs three campgrounds around the lake. Call (877) 444–6777 for reservations.

For more information: Alleghany Highlands Chamber of Commerce, 241 W. Main St., Covington, VA 24426; (540) 962–2178; www.alleghanyhighlands.com. Bath County Chamber of Commerce, (540) 839–5409; www.bathcountyva.org. Warm Springs Ranger District, Route 1, Box 30, Hot Springs, VA 24445; (540) 839–2521; www.fs.fed.us/r8/gwj/warmsprings/.

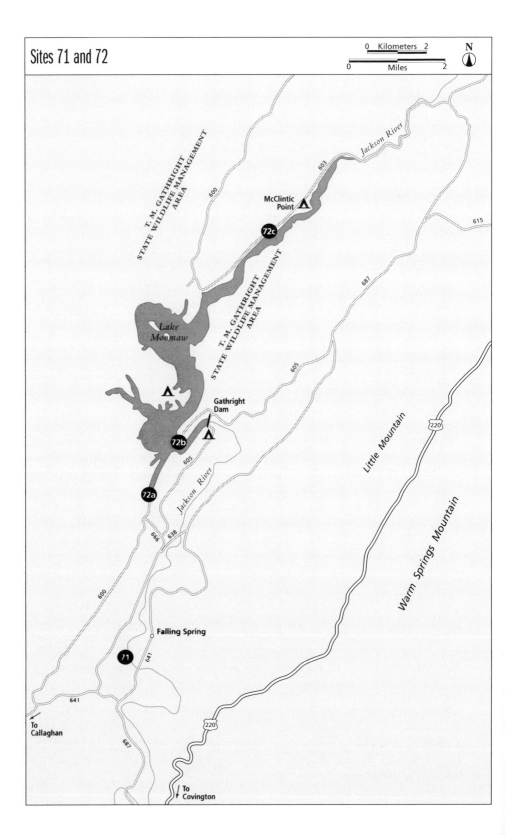

Sites 71 and 72

0   Kilometers   2

0   Miles   2

N

T. M. GATHRIGHT STATE WILDLIFE MANAGEMENT AREA

T. M. GATHRIGHT STATE WILDLIFE MANAGEMENT AREA

Jackson River

600

603

615

McClintic Point

72c

687

Lake Moomaw

605

Gathright Dam

Little Mountain

220

72b

605

Jackson River

72a

Warm Springs Mountain

695

638

600

Falling Spring

641

71

641

220

To Callaghan

687

To Covington

72 Lake Moomaw *(see map on page 116)*

Key species: Brown and rainbow trout, bass, yellow perch, sunfish, pickerel, catfish.

Best time to fish: All year.

Directions: From Covington, go north on Route 220 to Route 687 and follow the project signs to the dam site.

Description: Moomaw is the second-largest impounded lake in western Virginia, at about 2,500 acres. It is quite deep, over 150 feet, and supports both warm- and cold-water fisheries. Over 40 miles of wooded shoreline makes it an impressive place to spend a few days angling. No trout stamp or Forest Service permit is required in Moomaw.

The fishing: Yellow perch, which was introduced to the lake by accident, is doing very well. The state record (2 pounds, 7 ounces) was taken here. This is a great year-round fish. They are caught all winter long through the ice or by drifting.

Rainbow and brown trout are stocked yearly. Actually, two different strains of rainbow are found in Moomaw. The fish do well, and many 3-to-5-pounders are taken every year. Fishing is particularly good in the spring when the trout are gorging themselves with alewives.

Both small and largemouth bass are found in the lake. The smallies occupy the rocky area below the steep cliffs around McClintic and Coles Points. Bucket mouths are found on the shallow flats near the islands, Greenwood Point, and the swimming beach.

Panfish: Crappie and bluegills are other Moomaw success stories. A stocking of stunted specks yielded 2-pound fish in just a few years. Large bluegills and redears are also consistently taken.

Yellow bullheads and channel catfish are quite plentiful. The channels run up to over 20 pounds and 10-to-15-pounders are common.

Chain pickerel of 4 and 5 pounds are taken every year. They are so large that some call them pike. Look for shallow weedy areas especially in the midlake area. These guys will often hit surface plugs.

The best baits to use here are spinner baits, jigs, plastics, spoons, spinners and surface lures, crank baits, night crawlers, and live minnows.

Access: Two boat ramps are available at the south end of the lake. To get to the first, follow Route 600 north from Callaghan. The ramp is found at the end of the road (72a). The second can be reached by turning east on Route 666 from Route 600. Follow that north on Route 605 across Gathright Dam, then follow the signs to ramp (72b).

At the north end of the lake, a ramp is located at Bolar Flats. From Bacova, follow Route 687 south to Route 603 south. This road goes right by the access to the ramp (72c).

Camping: The USDA Forest Service runs three campgrounds around the lake. Call (877) 444–6777 for reservations.

Lake Moomaw produced the state record yellow perch (2 pds. 7 oz.).

For more information: Alleghany Highlands Chamber of Commerce, 241 W. Main St., Covington, VA 24426; (540) 962–2178; www.alleghanyhighlands.com. Bath County Chamber of Commerce, (540) 839–5409; www.bathcountyva.org. Warm Springs Ranger District, Route 1, Box 30, Hot Springs, VA 24445; (540) 839–2521; www.fs.fed.us/r8/gwj/warmsprings/.

A marina and bait-and-tackle shops include The Hitching Post, HCR-1, Box 151, Warm Springs, VA 24484; (540) 279–4179. Bolar Flats Marina, P.O. Box 812, Hot Springs, VA 24445; (540) 279–4144. The Bait Place, 707 E. Morris Hill Rd., Covington, VA 24426; (540) 965–0633.

73 St. Marys River

Key species: Brook trout.

Best time to fish: All year.

Directions: St. Marys River lies within the St. Marys Wilderness Area. From Steeles Tavern, take Route 56 southeast. Turn northeast on Route 608 then east on FR 42 to the junction of FR 41. Continue on 41 to trailheads.

Description: The St. Marys River flows through a beautiful and wild canyon. There is evidence of the time in the early 1900s when it was mined for manganese.

The fishing: This is a brook-trout stream. In the past, rainbows were present but they have died off and not been restocked. This is a single-hook, artificial-lure, and fly-fishing river. Check with the Virginia Department of Game and Inland Fisheries (VDGIF) for other regulations.

The best baits to use here are spinners, spoons, and small jigs. Use a single hook.

Fly patterns: Caddis larvae, stone flies, and various mayflies. Streamers and flashy marabous also work at times.

Access: There are trailheads at the lower parking lot, Mine Bank Branch, and Green Pond. Stop at one and start hiking.

Camping: The area is designated as wilderness and camping is therefore allowed. However, no facilities are available.

For more information: VDGIF, 517 Lee Hwy., P.O. Box 996, Verona, VA 24482; (540) 248–9360; www.dgif.virginia.gov/fishing/. United States Forest Service, Pedlar-Glenwood Ranger District, P.O. Box 10, Natural Bridge Station, VA 24579; (540) 291–2189; www.southernregion.fs.fed.us/gwj/.

74 The Maury River

Key species: Trout, bass, sunfish.

Best time to fish: October through May.

Directions: The Maury flows out of Lake Merriweather. Route 39 follows the river for a number of miles to the southeast.

From Lexington take Route 11 north (it crosses the Maury) and turn west on 631. This road follows the river for a few miles.

Out of Glasgow take Route 130 east. Turn north on Route 501, then west on 663. This follows the river for a number of miles.

Description: The Maury begins in the mountains of Rockbridge County. In fact, unlike most of Virginia's rivers, it is fully contained within a single county. The headwaters are quite fast, but areas of slow water are numerous. It is a short river flowing only about 30 miles before emptying into the James at Glasgow.

Areas of rapids and big boulders are common. Only the experienced should canoe or kayak this river.

The fishing: This river is stocked with trout during the colder months. Most of the uncaught trout do not make it through the summer because the river gets warm and shallow. Smallmouth bass and a few species of sunfish are quite abundant here and are at least as popular as the stocked trout. Many of the small creeks and brooks that enter the Maury have populations of native brook trout. Special regulations apply on bass and trout.

The best baits to use here are worms and packaged trout bait, spinners, spoons, and small jigs.

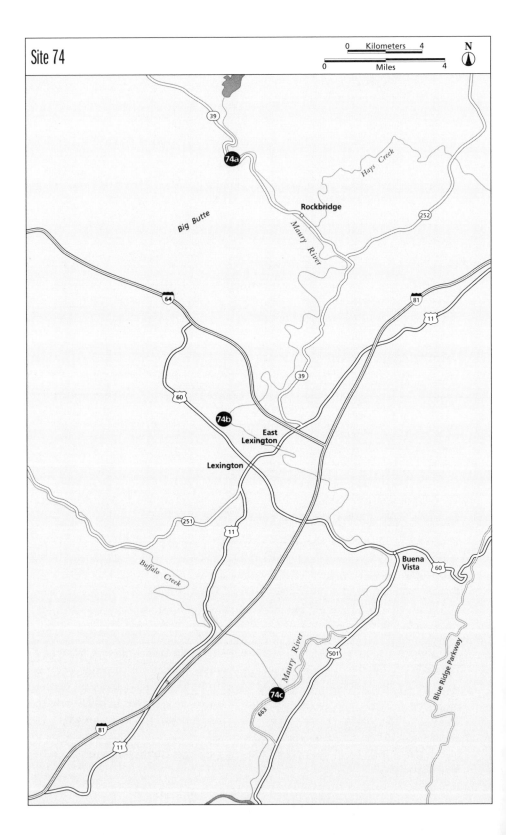

Fly patterns: Caddis larvae, stone flies and various mayflies. Streamers and flashy marabous also work at times.

Access: The Virginia Department of Game and Inland Fisheries (VDGIF) Goshen/Little North Mountain WMA parking area is located off Route 39. There's no sign—look for a dirt road on the left 1.1 miles south of Route 601.

The river flows out of Lake Merriweather. Route 39 follows the river for a number of miles to the southeast. Many good wading areas can be found along this stretch (74a).

Access can also be found by taking Route 11 north from Lexington to where it crosses the Maury. Turn west on 631, which follows the river for a few miles (74b).

If coming out of Glasgow, take Route 130 east. Turn north on Route 501, then west on Route 663, which follows the stream for a number of miles (74c).

Camping: Glen Maury Park, Buena Vista, (540) 261–7321 or (800) 555–8845; www.glenmaurypark.com. Lake A. Willis Robertson, 106 Lake Robertson Dr., Lexington, VA 24450; (540) 463–4164; www.co.rockbridge.va.us/departments/lake_robertson.htm. LEE HI Campground, 2516 N. Lee Hwy., Lexington, VA 24450; (540) 463–3478 or (800) 296–5344; www.leehi.com/dan%20html%20file/campground.htm.

For more information: Glenn Rose, James River Basin Canoe, 1870 E. Midland Trail, Lexington, VA 24450; (540) 261–7334; www.canoevirginia.com. VDGIF, 517 Lee Hwy., P.O. Box 996, Verona, VA 24482; (540) 248–9360; www.dgif.virginia.gov/fishing/.

75 The Pound River

Key species: Rainbow and brown trout.

Best time to fish: All year.

Directions: Routes 631 and 754 parallel the river above Flannagan Reservoir around the town of Flemington. Business Route 23 follows the river near the village of Pound.

Below Flannagan Dam, Route 739 runs alongside the river to its junction with the Russell Fork River.

Description: For 1.6 miles below Flannagan Dam, the Pound River is regulated for a stocked trout fishery.

The fishing: The first 0.4 mile below the dam is a Category A stocked trout stream. That means that six trout greater than 7 inches may be kept per day. The next 1.2 miles downstream to where the Pound empties into the Russell Fork River is a special regulation area. Only single-hook artificials are allowed, with a two-fish bag limit and a 16-inch minimum size.

Above Flannagan the Pound has a similar variety of fish as the reservoir. Walleye make a spring run up the river from the lake.

The best baits to use here are spinners, spoons, and small jigs. Use a single hook where it applies.

Fly patterns: Caddis larvae, stone flies and various mayflies. Streamers and flashy marabous also work at times.

Access: A few boat ramps can be found at Flannagan Reservoir. Take Route 63 north from Haysi. Turn west on Route 614 then north onto Route 739. Follow to the ramp. Another is located if you continue on Route 614 west to a ramp sign on the right. Turn north to the ramp.

Camping: John W. Flannagan Reservoir has three campgrounds, all operated by the U.S. Army Corps of Engineers. They are the Lower Twin, Cranesnest Areas #1, #2, and #3, and the Pound River Area. Contact the Corps for more information (see below).

For more information: John W. Flannagan Dam and Reservoir, Virginia Corps Projects, Route 1, Box 268, Haysi, VA 24256-9739; (540) 835–9544. Virginia Department of Game and Inland Fisheries' (VDGIF) regional office in Marion, Virginia, (540) 783–4860; www.dgif.virginia.gov/fishing/. Lots of information can also be found at www.dickensoncounty.net/johnflannagan.html.

76 Flannagan Reservoir

Key species: Large and smallmouth bass, walleye, hybrid bass, crappie, carp, catfish.

Best time to fish: March through January, but good fishing can also be had all winter long.

Description: Flannagan is a deep, clear lake. Sometimes one can see 20 feet below the surface. It is surrounded by hardwood forest with a surface area of over 1,100 acres.

Directions: From Haysi, take Route 63 north to Route 614 west, then 739 north. This leads to a ramp and the dam. From Route 23, take Route 83 east into Clintwood and turn north onto Main Street, which becomes Route 607. Turn north onto Route 614. A boat ramp will be found after the bridge near Tandy. Continuing on 614 and then north onto 739 will bring you to the ramp near the dam.

The fishing: Smallmouth bass are usually taken around the rocky cliffs of the lower reservoir, while bucket mouths are more likely encountered in Cranesnest Arm.

Walleye run up the rivers in the spring. Try the Pound and the Cranesnest. Later in the season they move back into the lake and take up residence around rocky banks. As the lake warms, most of the fish move into deeper water.

Panfishing for crappie and bluegill is excellent in Flannagan. A habitat enhancement project is at least in part responsible.

As in many other bodies of water, carp are an underutilized species. They grow very large in this lake—40-to-50-pounders are possible. To target carp, fish with corn or dough from the bank with a fish-finder rig.

Hybrid bass are very fast growing and a relatively new addition to Flannagan. Hybrids over 24 inches have been taken here.

The best baits to use in this area are lures that imitate herring and shad, live alewives and shad, spinner baits, jigs, and surface lures.

Fly patterns: Muddlers, leech and crawfish patterns, and deer-hair bugs. Poppers also work, as do alewife and shad patterns.

Access: Free boat ramps include the Cranesnest River Ramp and the Spillway Ramp, both useable when the water is high. Fee ramps include Junction Ramp (year-round access), next to the marina on Route 615; and Lower Twin Ramp and Pound River Ramp, both near the campground and both high-water ramps. Two wheelchair-accessible fishing piers are located at Cranesnest River Ramp and Spillway Ramp.

John W. Flannagan Boat Dock has docking facilities, fishing supplies, a gas station, and a snack bar. It is located at the Junction Area. Call (540) 835–8408 for more information.

Camping: John W. Flannagan Reservoir has three campgrounds, all operated by the U.S. Army Corps of Engineers. They are the Lower Twin, Cranesnest Areas #1, #2, and #3, and the Pound River Area. Contact the Corps for more information (see below).

For more information: John W. Flannagan Dam and Reservoir, Virginia Corps Projects, Route 1, Box 268, Haysi, VA 24256-9739; (540) 835–9544. Virginia Department of Game and Inland Fisheries' (VDGIF) regional office in Marion, Virginia, (540) 783–4860; www.dgif.virginia.gov/fishing/. Lots of information is also available at www.dickensoncounty.net/johnflannagan.html.

77 The New River

Key species: Smallmouth, spotted, largemouth, rock, striped, white, and hybrid striped bass, muskellunge, walleye, black crappie, channel catfish, flathead catfish, yellow perch, redbreast sunfish, bluegill.

Best time to fish: March through November.

Directions: The New River runs for many miles through southwestern Virginia. To get to one of the main sections, take Interstate 81 east out of Wytheville. Turn south onto Interstate 77. This crosses the river at Jackson Ferry, very close to a section of the New River State Park. Follow directions below for accesses.

Description: The New River is unusual in that it flows in a northward direction. It starts in North Carolina, crosses into Virginia near Mouth of Wilson, meanders a few miles, and then crosses back into North Carolina. The river reenters Virginia, hugs the border, then passes through Carroll, Wythe, and Pulaski Counties before empting into Claytor Lake. After leaving Claytor, the river runs into West Virginia and eventually becomes a tributary of the Mississippi. For most of its journey, the New is surrounded by magnificent scenery. Areas of Class II and III rapids often give way to slow, deep sections.

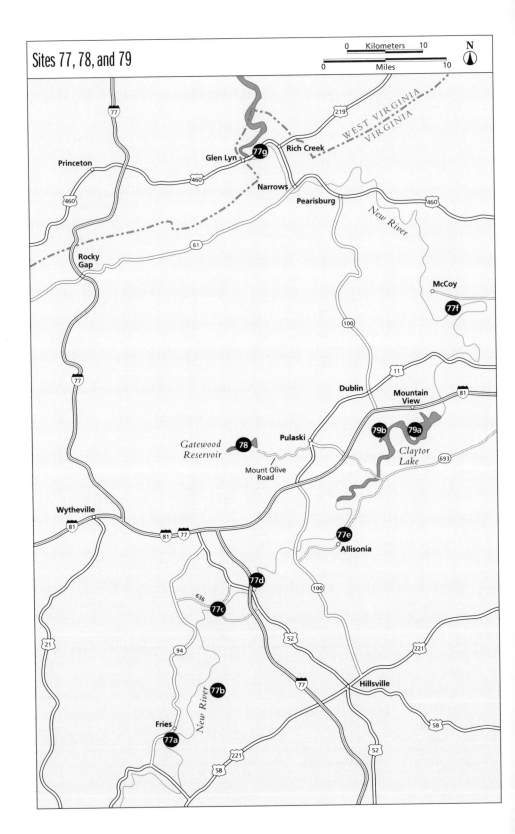

Sites 77, 78, and 79

Kilometers 0 — 10

Miles 0 — 10

N

Princeton

West Virginia / Virginia

219

Glen Lyn **77g** Rich Creek

460

Narrows

Pearisburg

New River

460

McCoy

77f

Rocky Gap

61

100

77

Dublin

11

Mountain View

81

79b **79a**

Pulaski

Claytor Lake

693

Gatewood Reservoir **78**

Mount Olive Road

Wytheville

81

81 77

77e

Allisonia

77d

636

77c

100

94

52

21

77b

77

Hillsville

New River

58

Fries

77a

221

52

58

Live gizzard shad are used for striped bass in the New River.

The fishing: If the New River is not the best river to fish in Virginia, it is close. Just about every freshwater species is available and many state records have been caught in this stream.

Fishing for a trophy smallmouth bass is best in March, April, or May. While bigmouths are available in many sections of the river, many trophy fish are caught between Claytor Lake and the West Virginia border.

The state record walleye was taken from the New. The best walleye fishing is from February through May. Two hot spots are frequented by serious pike-perch anglers: Fosters Falls and Buck Dam. To access the first area, two boat ramps are located in Fosters Falls Village. A bank-fishing access point is located at Buck Dam near Austinville at the end of Route 636. Spinner/minnow combos work well, as do plastic, grubs, and minnow jigs.

The state record muskie came from the New River. The Virginia Department of Game and Inland Fisheries (VDGIF) stocks these large predators at most boat landings from the North Carolina state line to Fries Dam and again from Claytor Lake Dam to West Virginia. The current Virginia state record, a 45-pound trophy, was caught in the lower New River in July 1989.

Flathead and channel catfish are found throughout the river. Some of the best areas are just below Claytor Dam and below Pepper's Ferry Bridge (Route 114). Above Claytor Lake, Foster's Falls to Allisonia and the Baywood and Independence sections in Grayson County are productive.

Great panfishing is found throughout the river. Don't overlook the side streams.

The best baits to use here are night crawlers, crawdads, live minnows or leeches, minnow- and crawfish-imitating artificials, buzz baits, jigs, and plastics.

Fly patterns: Any pattern that looks like a minnow, flashy streamers, and bass poppers.

Special regulations: Be sure to check with the VDGIF (see below) for current regulations on bass and walleye.

Access: There's a VDGIF boat ramp on river-left off Route 94 at Riverside Park in the town of Fries (77a).

Another ramp is located at Byllesby Dam at the end of Route 739 near River Hill (77b).

More ramps are available in Austinville at the Route 636 bridge (77c), in New River Trail State Park in Foster Falls Village (77d), in Allisonia off Route 693 (77e), and at Dedmon Sports Complex at Radford University.

There are developed VDGIF boat landings off Route 623 in Whitethorne (77f), on the right bank just below Narrows Falls, and at a beautiful small park above the Route 460 bridge in Glen Lyn (77g).

In addition to the above, many informal canoe takeouts are available. Numerous possible float trips and other takeouts are described at this Web site: www.dgif .virginia.gov/fishing/waterbodies/display.asp?id=163&section=maps.

Camping: New River Trail State Park parallels the river for 39 miles and operates five campgrounds. New River Trail State Park, 176 Orphanage Dr., Foster Falls, VA 24360; (276) 699–6778; www.dcr.state.va.us/parks/newriver.htm.

For more information: VDGIF, 1796 Hwy. 16, Marion, VA 24354; (276) 783–4860; www.dgif.virginia.gov/fishing/.

78 Gatewood Reservoir *(see map on page 124)*

Key species: Big bluegills, redear sunfish, bass, channel catfish, crappie.

Best time to fish: March through November.

Directions: Head west out of Pulaski on West Main Street, make a right on Magazine Street, then go left on Mount Olivet Road to the park entrance.

Description: Gatewood is in the national forest and is owned by the city of Pulaski. Its waters are clear and cover about 160 acres. Boats are allowed from April to October, but bank fishing is legal year-round. It's a pretty place to bring the family. Only electric motors are allowed.

The fishing: Big bluegills and redear sunfish are the main attraction at this mountain lake. Use grubs, worms, or flies. Largemouth bass to 10 pounds and smallies up to

Gatewood Reservoir is renowned for big bluegills.

3 pounds are taken regularly. Large channel cats up to 20 pounds are also available. The crappie fishery in Gatewood is also good.

The best baits to use here are jigs, plastics, surface lures, crank baits, night crawlers, crawfish, and live minnows.

Fly patterns: Mosquito patterns, deer-hair bugs, and leeches.

Access: This area has no boat ramp, but anglers are allowed to launch by hand. Boat rentals are available between April and October.

Camping: Both formal camping and wilderness camping are available at the park.

For more information: Gatewood Park, (540) 980–2561. Pulaski County Parks and Recreation Department office, (540) 994–8624; www.pulaskicounty.org/pcrec/. Pulaski County Chamber of Commerce, 4440 Cleburne Blvd., Dublin, VA 24084; (540) 674–1991; www.pulaskichamber.info.

79 Claytor Lake (see map on page 124)

Key species: Largemouth, smallmouth, striped, hybrid, white, and spotted bass.

Best time to fish: March through January, but good fishing can also be had all winter long.

Directions: Almost all the exits heading east off Interstate 81 between Pulaski and Radford lead to the lake.

Description: This 4,000-plus-acre lake is the result of an impoundment of the New River. It is surrounded by steep rocky slopes and is very picturesque.

The fishing: Some years, smallmouth and spotted bass are more numerous than bucket mouths. These fish prefer crawfish, leeches, and other invertebrates. Largemouth bass are fish eaters and many use live shad and alewives or imitations. Striped and hybrid bass do really well in this lake, with many citations taken. Shad and alewives are the favored bait but some use popping lures when the fish are breaking water. A few large walleyes from earlier stockings are still taken. Crappie, catfish, and bluegill are fairly easy to catch here.

The best baits to use here are lures that imitate herring and shad, spinner baits, plastics, and live minnows.

Fly patterns: For black bass, use muddlers, leech and crawfish patterns, and deer-hair bugs. Poppers also work. For striped and hybrid bass, use alewife and shad patterns.

Access: The Virginia Department of Game and Inland Fisheries (VDGIF) maintains boat ramps on Route 693 in Allisonia (77e), at Claytor State Park south of Mountain View (79a), and in Harry DeHaven Park on West Poor House Road (79b). In addition, the state park also has a ramp, and a number of commercial ramps are also available.

There's a wheelchair-accessible fishing pier in Harry DeHaven Park at Harry's Point. Many of the lake's species can be caught here throughout the year. Anglers may encounter striped bass and hybrid striped bass during the cold months.

The Rock House Marina is located at 3776 Rock House Rd., Pulaski, VA 24301; (540) 980–1488 (marina); www.rockhousemarina.com/files.

Camping and other accommodations: Claytor Lake State Park, 6620 Ben H. Bolen Drive, Dublin, VA 24084; (540) 643–2500 or (800) 933–PARK; www.dcr.state.va .us/parks/claytor.htm. A lot of information about accommodations can be found at http://claytor-lake.net/real-estate/for-rent/. The state park also has cabins for rent.

For more information: Pulaski County Chamber of Commerce, 4440 Cleburne Blvd., Dublin, VA 24084; (540) 674–1991; www.pulaskichamber.info/officers.htm. VDGIF, 1796 Highway 16, Marion, VA 24354; (276) 783-4860; www.dgif. virginia.gov/fishing/.

80 Smith Mountain Lake

Key species: Large and smallmouth bass, catfish, striped bass.

Best time to fish: March through January, but good fishing can also be had all winter long.

Sites 80 and 81

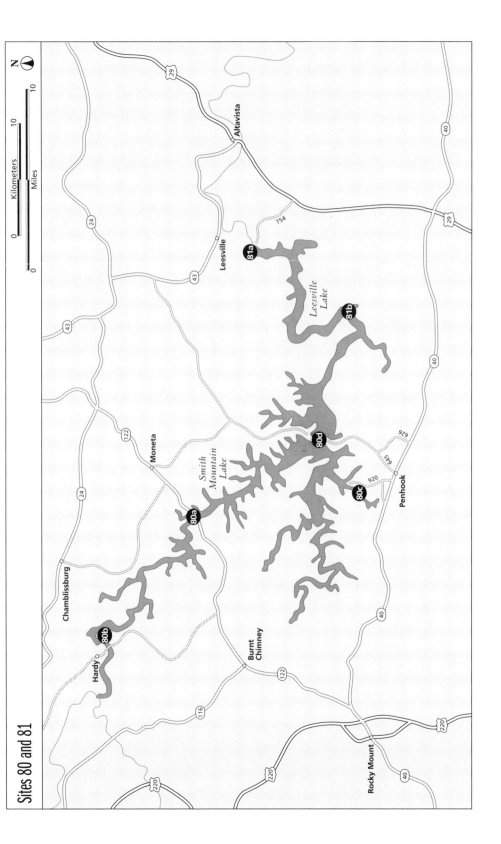

Directions: From Roanoke, take Route 116 south to Route 122 east at Burnt Chimney. Follow Route 122 to lake.

Description: This lake is one of Virginia's premier fishing holes. It is large: over 20,000 acres with over 500 miles of shoreline. Smith Mountain is not very far from Lynchburg, Roanoke, and Danville, and facilities abound around the lake.

The fishing: Smith Mountain Lake is known for its striped-bass fishery. Forty-pound fish are a possibility and lots of 15-to-20-pound fish are caught. During the hottest part of the summer, most of the line-siders are found in the southern and eastern parts of the lake. However, for most of the year, they are available throughout the waterway.

Bucket mouths are the most popular species of fish in the lake but many also fish for their smaller cousins, smallmouths. Two-to-four-pound fish are common. The best bass fishing is upstream of the dam. Most take advantage of both natural and man-made cover.

The catfish population is composed of flatheads, channels, and whites. The lake has good populations of all of them.

Crappie and bluegill panfish are also available. The 'gills are rather small but some large crappies are taken.

The best baits to use here are live shad, minnows, surface lures, night crawlers, and jigs.

Fly patterns: streamers resembling shad.

Access: Boat ramps are abundant around Smith Mountain Lake. There's a concrete ramp at the bridge on Route 122.

Another ramp is located at Hardy Ford (80b). From Hardy, take Route 634 south to ramp.

To reach the Penhook concrete ramp from Penhook, take Route 660 north and turn north on Route 920 (80c).

To reach the Anthony Ford concrete ramp from Penhook, take Route 645 north, then head north on Route 626 (80d).

In addition, just about all the campgrounds and the state park have at least one ramp. A barrier-free fishing pier is also available at the state park.

Camping: Blue Ridge Campground, 8131 Burnt Chimney Rd. (Route 670), Wirtz, VA 24184; (540) 721–3866. Crazy Horse Campground/Marina, 400 Crazy Horse Dr., Moneta, VA 24121; (540) 721–2792. Eagle's Roost Campground, 15335 Smith Mountain Lake Pkwy., Huddleston, VA 24104; (540) 297–7381. Smith Mountain Lake State Park, 1235 State Park Rd., Huddleston, VA 24104-9547; (540) 297–6066; www.dcr.state.va.us/parks/smithmtn.htm.

For more information: Smith Mountain Lake Visitors Center, Bridgewater Plaza, 16430 Booker T. Washington Hwy. #2, Moneta, VA 24121; (800) 676–8203; visitsmithmountainlake.com. Virginia Department of Game and Inland Fisheries

(VDGIF), 1132 Thomas Jefferson Rd., Forest, VA 24551; (434) 525–7522; www.dgif.virginia.gov/fishing/.

81 Leesville Lake *(see map on page 129)*

Key species: Striped bass, white bass, walleye.

Best time to fish: March through January, but good fishing can also be had all winter long.

Directions: From Altavista, take Business Route 29 southwest to Route 29 south. Turn west on Shula Drive to NW Gallows Road (Route 754). Take this road to the ramp and dam.

Description: This lake has low productivity but contains a good population of predators. One problem is that water levels might vary as much as 10 feet in a day. Leesville is over 3,000 acres and has very little development along the shoreline. It is a good place to get away from it all.

The fishing: Some very large striped bass are taken here. In fact, the Virginia state record was caught in Leesville. Walleyes grow well here and an excellent population of white bass swims this lake's waters.

   The best baits to use here are live minnows, night crawlers, spinner baits, and plastics.

Fly patterns: For striped bass, Black Phantom and any shad pattern.

Access: There are Virginia Department of Game and Inland Fisheries (VDGIF) ramps at Leesville Dam #7 off Route 754 (81a) and at Myers Creek off Route 768 (81b).

Camping: Blue Ridge Campground, 8131 Burnt Chimney Rd. (Route 670), Burnt Chimney, VA 24184; (540) 721–3866. Crazy Horse Campground/Marinas, 400 Crazy Horse Dr., Moneta, VA 24121; (540) 721–2792. Eagle's Roost Campground, 15335 Smith Mountain Lake Pkwy., Huddleston, VA 24104; (540) 297–7381. Smith Mountain Lake State Park, 1235 State Park Rd., Huddleston, VA 24104-9547; (540) 297–6066; www.dcr.state.va.us/parks/smithmtn.htm.

For more information: Smith Mountain Lake Visitors Center, Bridgewater Plaza, 16430 Booker T. Washington Hwy. #2, Moneta, VA 24121; (800) 676–8203; visitsmithmountainlake.com. VDGIF, 1132 Thomas Jefferson Rd., Forest, VA 24551; (434) 525–7522; www.dgif.virginia.gov/fishing/.

82 Philpott Reservoir

Key species: Large and smallmouth bass, walleye, crappie, white catfish.

Best time to fish: March through January, but good fishing can also be had all winter long.

Directions: To get to the lower part of Philpott from Basset, take Route 57 west to Route 904 north and follow the signs.

Description: This reservoir is owned by the U.S. Army Corps of Engineers. There's no development along its shores, making it a nice place to get away to.

The fishing: While largemouth bass outnumber their smallmouth cousins in Philpott, many anglers concentrate on the latter. Some real trophies are caught. These fish are primarily found in the lower end of the lake, but bucket mouths are evenly distributed. Walleyes do quite well in this reservoir. Many are on the small side, 16 to 21 inches, but an occasional 6-to-8-pounder is caught. Crappies are not as numerous as in other lakes but they do grow to over 12 inches. White catfish are abundant in the lower end of the reservoir. Channel cats are also present and distributed throughout the lake.

The best baits to use here are spinner baits, plastics, and live minnows.

Fly patterns: Muddlers and deer-hair bugs.

Access: Numerous boat ramps and picnic areas are located around the lake. For a list, contact the Army Corps of Engineers (see below).

Camping: Fairy Stone State Park, 967 Fairystone Lake Dr., Stuart, VA 24171-9588; (276) 930–2424; www.dcr.state.va.us/parks/fairyst.htm.

The Army Corps of Engineers runs a number of campgrounds around Philpott. For more information, contact Philpott Lake–Virginia Corps Projects, Route 6, Box 140, Bassett, VA 24055-8617; (703) 629–2703; http://gorp.away.com/gorp/resource/us_nra/ace/va_phil.htm.

For more information: Contact the U.S. Army Corps of Engineers at (804) 738–6371 to determine water levels in the lake. Patrick County Chamber of Commerce, 212 Johnson St., P.O. Box 577, Stuart, VA 24171; (276) 694–6012; www.patrickchamber.com/index.cfm?pg=home. Martinsville and Henry County Chamber of Commerce, 115 Broad St., P.O. Box 709, Martinsville, VA 24114; (276) 632–6401; www.martinsville.com.

83 Bark Camp Lake

Key species: Brown and rainbow trout, largemouth bass, sunfish, catfish.

Best time to fish: All year.

Directions: Located in northern Scott County, take Alternate Route 58 north toward Tacoma from Dungannon, turn on Route 706 to Route 822, then take FR 993 to the lake. A parking fee is charged by the Forest Service.

Description: This clear-water lake is surrounded by forests and is very picturesque. It is owned by the Virginia Department of Game and Inland Fisheries (VDGIF) and covers about 61 acres.

The fishing: Bark Camp Lake is popular because of the stockings of trout, which take place from October through May. The lake has a good population of big-mouths, most over average size. Sunfish anglers will encounter a large variety: Bluegills, redear, warmouths, redbreast, and pumpkinseed are present. While not known for catfish, some very large channels are caught here.

The best baits to use here are spinner baits, jigs, plastics, spoons, spinners, surface lures, night crawlers, and live minnows.

Special regulations: Be sure to check on regulations for bass, trout stamp require-ments, a Forest Service license, and fishing hours.

Camping: Camping is available for anglers and others. Contact the Clinch Ranger District for information (see below).

Access: There's a paved boat ramp with parking available, as well as a wheelchair-accessible fishing pier.

For more information: Clinch Ranger District, 9416 Darden Dr., Wise, VA 24293; (276) 328–2931; www.fs.fed.us/r8/gwj/clinch/recreation/day_use/bark_camp_day use.shtml.

84 The Clinch River

Key species: Smallmouth and spotted bass, sauger, walleye, catfish.

Best time to fish: March through November.

Directions: From Clinchport, Route 65 south follows the river to the junction of Route 625, which then parallels the stream west to the Tennessee border. North of Clinchport, Route 65 more or less follows the river to Dungannon, where Route 72 north takes over this job. In Saint Paul, Route 640 south tracks the Clinch for a few miles, as do Route 654 west and Route 661 east out of Cleveland. Routes 637 and 641 south and west out of Gardner also follow the upper portions of the river for a distance.

Description: The Clinch River runs through Tennessee and Virginia. It meanders about 135 miles through some of the most spectacular scenery of the southwestern region of the state. It has some very wild sections and supports one of the largest diversities of freshwater mussels and over a hundred species of fish.

The fishing: The Clinch supports a wide variety of game fish. The most sought-after species are smallmouth and, though not plentiful, sauger. In fact, this river is the only body of water in Virginia where this walleye relative is found. Musky and wall-eye are also available, but they are scarce. Channel cats are abundant, and some good-size flatheads are also caught.

Suckers and carp are in good supply. Fish from the bank using sliding sinker bottom rigs with corn or dough. Bank fishing from the many access points is pos-sible. Some may prefer float trips.

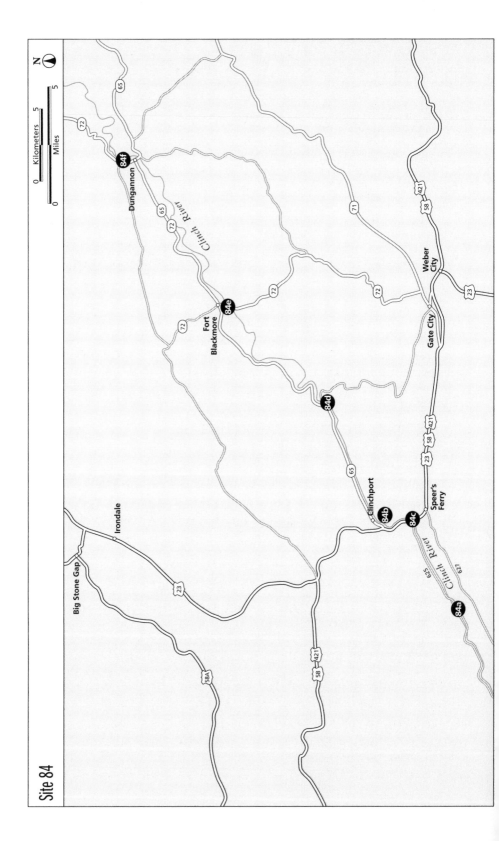

Site 84

The best baits to use here are night crawlers, crawdads, and live minnows or leeches. Deep-diving crank baits work well in deeper sections for smallies, walleye, and musky.

Fly patterns: This is a great river for fly-fishing. It can be waded in spots. Try any pattern that looks like a minnow, crawfish, or leech.

Access: There are many access points, including the State Line access point off Route 627 between the Tennessee border and Speer's Ferry (84a); Clinchport, which has the only boat ramp and is found off Route 65 north of the junction with Route 42 (84b); Speer's Ferry Access, a bit north of Speer's Ferry on Route 421 (84c); Hill Station on Route 645 just off Route 65 (84d); Fort Blackmore on Route 72 just south of Route 65 (84e); and Dungannon on Route 65 near town (84f).

Camping and lodging: Natural Tunnel State Park, Route 3, Box 250, Duffield, VA 24244-9361; (276) 940–2674; www.dcr.state.va.us/parks/naturalt.htm. Rikemo Lodge, Dungannon; (866) RIKEMO–8.

For more information: Virginia Department of Game and Inland Fisheries (VDGIF), 1796 Hwy. 16, Marion, VA 24354; (276) 783–4860; fax (276) 783–6115; www.dgif.virginia.gov/fishing/. This Web site describes a number of float trips on the Clinch: www.dgif.virginia.gov/fishing/waterbodies/display.asp?id=147 &section=maps.

85 The North Fork of the Holston River

Key species: Smallmouth bass, catfish, carp, sunfish.

Best time to fish: March through November.

Directions: From Marion take Route 16 north. It crosses the North Fork near Chatham Hill. Take Route 42 east. It follows the river for a ways.

Description: This river runs for over 100 miles in southwestern Virginia. It begins in Bland County and crosses into Tennessee near Yuma.

The fishing: The North Fork of the Holston is one of the best rivers to attempt to catch a trophy smallie. Great opportunities to catch numerous carp, flatheads, and sunfish are found throughout the river.

The best baits to use here are night crawlers, crawdads, live minnows or leeches, minnow-imitating artificials, and plastics.

Fly patterns: Any pattern that looks like a minnow, crawfish, or leech. Bass poppers.

Special regulations: Be sure to check with the Virginia Department of Game and Inland Fisheries (VDGIF, see below) for current regulations on bass. This river has been targeted to enhance its already fine population of smallmouths.

A mercury advisory on eating fish out of the North Fork is in effect. Check to ascertain whether this has changed.

Access: There are two good boat ramps near the town of Saltville. One is in town and the other is downstream off Route 611. Many roads follow the North Fork of the Holston River. Canoe- and foot-access points abound.

Camping and accommodations: Riverside Campground, 18496 North Fork River Rd., Abingdon, VA 24210; www.holidayjunction.com/usa/va/cva0004.html. Raven Ridge Campground & Retreat, 517 Hayters Gap Rd., Saltville, VA 24370; (276) 944–5024. Raven Ridge B&B, 21705 Raven Ridge, Saltville, VA 24370; (276) 944–5024. Saltville Inn, 525 E. Main St., Saltville, VA 24370; (276) 496–4444. River Garden Bed & Breakfast, 19080 North Fork River Rd., Abingdon, VA 24210; (276) 676–0335 or (800) 952–4296; www.bbonline.com/va/rivergarden/.

For more information: VDGIF, 1796 Hwy. 16, Marion, VA 24354; (276) 783–4860; www.dgif.virginia.gov/fishing/.

86 The South Fork of the Holston River

Key species: Rainbow and brown trout.

Best time to fish: All year. Autumn is a particularly good time to try for a trophy.

Directions: From Marion, take Interstate 81 west to Adwolf Road south, which ends at a tee with Riverside Road (Route 660). This follows the south fork for quite a distance. This road eventually intersects with Loves Mill Road (Route 762), which follows and crosses the river for a few miles. Eventually, it moves away from the river but crosses Route 714. Turn south and this road comes back to the south fork and follows it for a distance.

Description: This is one of the premier trout streams in Virginia. A few small streams combine near the town of Sugar Grove to form the South Fork of the Holston River. The stream flows southwest and eventually empties into South Holston Lake. Special regulations apply, so be sure to be familiar with them before fishing.

The fishing: From the national forest boundary to about 500 feet upstream of the dam at the Buller Fish Cultural Station, a creel limit of two fish per day with a 16-inch minimum size limit applies. Both rainbows and browns are present and only single-hook artificials are allowed.

A designated catch-and-release fishing area is within the boundaries of the Virginia Department of Game and Inland Fisheries' (VDGIF) Buller Station. Only single-hook artificial lures may be used and all fish must be released immediately.

Two stocked areas are located below the Buller property. One is around the Thomas Bridge area and the other is found along Riverside Road in the St. Clair Bottom area. A trout license as well as a statewide freshwater fishing license is required here.

The best baits to use here are spinners, spoons, and small jigs. Use a single hook where it applies.

Fly patterns: Caddis larvae, stone flies, and various mayflies. Streamers and flashy marabous also work at times.

Access: Access is relatively easy as many roads run along this river.

Camping: Hungry Mother Campgrounds Inc., 2287 Park Blvd., Marion, VA 24354; (276) 783–2046. Mount Rogers National Recreation Area, 3714 Hwy. 16, Marion, VA 24354-4097; (276) 783–5196; www.fs.fed.us/r8/gwj/mr/.

For more information: VDGIF, 1796 Hwy. 16, Marion, VA 24354; (276) 783–4860; www.dgif.virginia.gov/fishing/.

87 The Middle Fork of the Holston River

Key species: Redbreast sunfish, smallmouth bass, bluegill, rock bass, and an occasional largemouth, walleye, catfish, or crappie. The upper portion is stocked with trout during the colder months.

Best time to fish: All year.

Directions: The Middle Fork of the Holston runs through Marion. It starts in Smyth County and empties into South Holston Reservoir in Washington County. It parallels Interstate 81 for quite a distance.

Description: This river in southwestern Virginia flows approximately 56 miles through Smyth and Washington Counties. Parts of it are navigable, but much of the lower portion is not accessible as it is privately owned.

The fishing: There is a wide variety of fishing opportunities. Trout are stocked near the towns of Atkins and Marion in the upper part of the river. This is primarily done through the colder months. Be sure to read the signs and regulations. Some areas may require a trout stamp. Within the town limits of Marion is a universally accessible fishing pier.

Redbreast sunfish, rock bass, and bluegills are abundant below the trout-fishing areas in the navigable areas in Smyth and Washington Counties. Sixteen-to-twenty-inch smallmouths are plentiful, and walleye make spawning runs out of South Holston Reservoir in March and April. Largemouth bass, black crappie, and channel cats may also be caught.

The best baits to use here are worms, packaged trout bait, spinners, spoons, and small jigs. Use a single hook where it applies.

Fly patterns: Caddis larvae, stone flies, and various mayflies. Streamers and flashy marabous also work at times. Small poppers and bream busters.

Access points: Access is very limited to the lower portion of the river due to private land. Some may be found at bridge crossings. There's a wheelchair-accessible fishing pier within the Marion town limits.

Camping: Hungry Mother Campgrounds Inc., 2287 Park Blvd., Marion, VA 24354; (276) 783–2046. Mount Rogers National Recreation Area, 3714 Hwy. 16, Marion, VA 24354-4097; (276) 783–5196; www.fs.fed.us/r8/gwj/mr/.

For more information: Virginia Department of Game and Inland Fisheries (VDGIF), 1796 Hwy. 16, Marion, VA 24354; (276) 783–4860; www.dgif.virginia.gov/fishing/.

Water-level information is available at this Web site: http://nwis.waterdata.usgs .gov/va/nwis/uv?dd_cd=01&dd_cd=03&format=gif&period=31&site_no=03474000.

88 South Holston Reservoir

Key species: Large and smallmouth bass, walleye, crappie, catfish.

Best time to fish: All year.

Directions: From Interstate 81 in Abingdon, turn south on Route 75 then east on Route 670.

Description: South Holston Reservoir straddles the Virginia-Tennessee border. About 1,600 acres are on the Old Dominion side. As of this writing, no reciprocal agreement has been signed. Be sure you do not wander over to the Tennessee side unless you hold a license for that state.

The fishing: Smallmouth bass are pursued more than largemouths in South Holston. However, there are plenty of bigmouths on the Virginia side. Anglers employ a very unique technique in South Holston during the winter. They fish with a hair jig about 10 feet under a float. This keeps the bait at the right depth.

Walleye are doing very well in this lake. March is one of the best times to fish for this species. Walleyes spawn in the Middle Fork and South Fork of the Holston Rivers. This takes place in late winter and early spring. They return to the lake in May. Crank baits cast at night is a favorite method.

Crappie fishing is excellent in South Holston. Many fish in the 10-to-15-inch range are caught. Look for submerged brush.

The most abundant catfish is the channel. They provide good sport for anglers fishing from shore. Some very nice flatheads roam the depths of South Holston. Fish the rocky bluffs with live bait or lures that imitate small fish.

The best baits to use here are lures that imitate herring and shad, live alewives and shad, crawlers, and hair jigs under floats in the winter.

Fly patterns: Deer-hair bugs, leech, and alewife and shad patterns.

Access: There are Virginia Department of Game and Inland Fisheries (VDGIF) ramps in Avens on Route 672 and in Whitaker Hollow Park on Route 664.

There are fee ramps in Washington County Park near the Tennessee state line.

Sportsman's Marina has ramps and other facilities. To get there, take Route 75 west out of Abingdon to Bowman Road. Go south and then turn east on Lake

Road. Turn south on Sportsman Drive and follow it to the marina (23511 Sportsman Drive, Abingdon, VA 24211; 276-628-2850).

Camping and other accommodations: Washington County Park Authority, Valley Street Office Building, 234 W. Valley St., Suite A, Abingdon VA 24210; (276) 676–6215; www.washcova.com/departments/park_auth/. Callebs Cove Campground, 25136 Whitaker Hollow Rd., Abingdon VA 24211; (276) 475–5222; www.callebscovecampground.com.

For a list of B&Bs, visit www.washingtonvachamber.org/bedandbreak.htm. For a list of cabin rentals and lodges, visit www.washingtonvachamber.org/cottages.htm.

For more information: VDGIF, 1796 Hwy. 16, Marion, VA 24354; (276) 783–4860; www.dgif.virginia.gov/fishing/. Bristol Welcome Center, I–81, 66 Island Rd., Bristol, VA 24201; (276) 466–2932. Abingdon Convention & Visitors Bureau, 335 Cummings St., Abingdon, Virginia 24210; (276) 676–2282; www.abingdon.com/tourism.

89 The Whitetop Laurel Creek

Key species: Rainbows, brookies, brown trout.

Best time to fish: All year.

Directions: From Damascus, take Route 58 east. This road follows the creek. Where the creek swings away from the road, the Virginia Creeper Trail follows the stream. Follow signs to the parking areas and the Virginia Creeper Trail. Maps and trail information are available at the parking areas.

Heading west out of Damascus, Route 58 more or less parallels the creek to the point where it runs into the South Fork of the Holston.

Description: Whitetop Laurel is a beautiful wild-trout stream. Located in Washington County, it has wheelchair-accessible areas so everyone can wet a line.

The fishing: About a 7-mile section of this river is stocked with trout and about 5 miles is a special-regulations area. In the winter most fly-fishers use nymph patterns: tiny caddis larvae to giant black stoneflies. During warm weather blue-wing olive mayfly hatch and dry flies can be used.

The best baits to use here are worms, packaged trout bait, spinners, spoons, and small jigs. Use a single hook where it applies.

Fly patterns: For nymph patterns, caddis larvae, stone flies, and various mayflies. Streamers and flashy marabous also work at times.

Special regulations: Areas of the Whitetop Laurel have different regulations. Be sure to know where you are fishing and what the rules are. Check with the Virginia Department of Game and Inland Fisheries (VDGIF).

Camping: Camping is allowed in the national forest sections of the river.

For more information: VDGIF, 1796 Hwy. 16, Marion, VA 23454; (540) 783–4860; www.dgif.virginia.gov/fishing/. The Town of Damascus, P.O. Box 56, Damascus, VA 24236; (540) 475–3831; www.damascus.org. Mount Rogers National Recreation Area, 3714 Hwy. 16, Marion, VA 24354; (276) 783–5196 or (800) 628–7202; www.fs.fed.us/r8/gwj/mr/.

Trout Fishing

The trout season is open year-round in Virginia. The best fishing is in the spring and autumn and during mild winter periods. Midsummer sees a large increase in water temperatures and low stream flows. This makes angling more difficult. However, persistence will result in adequate catches for experienced trout anglers even during the hot months.

Virginia has a large variety of habitat and some of the western areas of the state support natural populations of trout. To be specific, conditions for trout survival exist in over 2,000 miles of streams and rivers in the Old Dominion. Much of the rest of the state's waters become too hot and therefore too low in oxygen in the summer to sustain any salmonids.

The Virginia Department of Game and Inland Fisheries (VDGIF) has a variety of programs to provide trout to most areas of the state. These are:

- The Catchable-trout Stocking Program
- Delayed Harvest Trout Streams
- Fee Trout-fishing Areas
- The Fingerling Stocking Program
- The Wild Trout Program
- Trout Heritage Day Program

The Catchable-trout Stocking Program

This plan provides trout not only to areas where they may survive through the summer but also to lowland ponds and streams that just get too warm. Legal-size trout are stocked in these waters periodically throughout the cold months. It is expected that most will be caught before the water becomes too warm. How and when these waters are stocked is subject to change. For current schedules, see the Web site for the Department of Game and Inland Fisheries (VDGIF) at www.dgif.state.va .us/fishing/trout/.

These waters are not marked on maps because they are quite well known. Brief directions are provided to some below. For more information, contact the VDGIF or local bait shops in the area you want to fish.

Catchable-trout Stocking Waters

County	Stocked Waters	Directions
Albemarle	Mint Springs Lake (Upper)	From Charlottesville, take Rte. 250 west to Rte. 240 west to Rte. 788 west to Rte. 684 north to park.
	Moormans River	Take Rte. 614 out of White Hall. Access is near the Sugar Hollow Reservoir.
	Sugar Hollow Reservoir	Same as above.

Alleghany	Clifton Forge Reservoir	Take Rte. 606 north from Clifton Forge to Rte. 504.
	Jerrys Run	Take the Jerry's Run exit (exit 1) off Rte. 64 and turn left (south) onto FR 69.
	Pounding Mill Creek	From Covington, take Rte. 625 to FR 125.
	Smith Creek	From Clifton Forge, take Rte. 606 north past Rte. 504.
Amherst	Davis Mill Creek	From Oronoco, take Rte. 634 north to Coffee Town.
	Little Irish Creek	From Blue Ridge Pkwy., take FR 311 west.
	Pedlar River (Below dam)	Follow above to FR 39.
	Pedlar River (Lower)	From Peddler Mills, Rte. 643 north, Rte. 635 south, Rte. 702 west.
	Pedlar River (Upper)	
	Piney River	
	South Fork and Proper Rocky Row Run	From Alhambra, 745 and 63 west and 827 south.
Appomattox	Holliday Creek	From Rose Bower on Rte. 24 take 626 east.
Augusta	Back Creek	Out of Hebron, Routes 707, 708, and 841 all cross Back Creek.
	Braley Pond	
	Elkhorn Lake	From Rte. 250, take Rte. 715 north to FR 96.
	Falls Hollow	
	Hearthstone Lake	Stokesville, take Rte. 718 north to FR 101.
	Lower Sherando Lake	From Love, take Rte. 814 north to FR 91 west.
	Mills Creek	
	North River	From Elkhorn Lake, take FR 95 north to FR 985 east.
	South River (Ridgeview Park)	From Buena Vista, take Rte. 705 north to Rte. 608 east.
	South River	
	Upper Sherando Lake	
Bath	Back Creek	From Mountain Grove, take Rte. 600 north.
	Bullpasture River	Near Flood Rte. 678 south and 678 north, a number of crossroads to the east go to the Bullpasture.
	Douthat Lake/Wilson Creek	
	Jackson River (Hidden Valley)	
	Jackson River (Rte. 623)	From Rte. 220, take Rte. 623 south.
	Pads Creek	
	Spring Run	
Bedford	Liberty Lake	From Bedford, head south on Route 122.

Bland	Laurel Fork Creek	
	Lick Creek	From Ceres on Rte. 42, go north on Rte. 625.
	Wolf Creek	From Bastian, head north on Rte. 52 and turn west on Rte. 614.
Botetourt	Jennings Creek	From Arcadia, head south on Rte. 614.
	McFalls Creek	From Peaks of Otter, head northwest on Rte. 43 and turn north on Rte. 618.
	Middle Creek	From Arcadia, head south on Rte. 614 and turn east on Rte. 618.
	North Creek	From Arcadia, head south on Rte. 614 and turn east on FR 59 (North Creek Rd.).
	Roaring Run	From Strom, take Rte. 621 north.
Buchanan	Dismal River	
	Russell Fork River	From Haysi, Routes 80 south and 613 north follow the river.
Carroll	Chestnut Creek	
	Crooked Creek	From Galax take Rte. 58/220 and cross the creek. Off Rte. 58, take Rte. 722 south to Rte. 713 west.
	Little Reed Island Creek	From Richardson, take Rte. 749 north to Rte. 760 south.
	Lovills Creek	From Orchard Gap, take Rte. 691 south.
	Stewarts Creek	From Lambsburg, take Rte. 696 southwest.
Craig	Barbours Creek	From Rte. 311, take Rte. 611 north to 617 north.
	Potts Creek	
Dickenson	Cranesnest River	
	Frying Pan Creek	From Haysi, take Rte. 80 south to Rte. 625 west to Rte. 600 south.
	Pound River (Flan. Dam)	
	Russell Fork (Haysi)	From Haysi, take Rte. 80 south.
	Russell Fork (Bartlick)	
Fairfax	Accotink Creek	Rte. 636 crosses the creek.
	Holmes Run	
Fauquier	Thompson WMA Pond	From Delaplane, take Rte. 17 north to Rte. 688 west.
Floyd	Burkes Fork	From Rte. 221, take Rte. 758 south to 784 east to 785 south.
	Goose Creek	From Rte. 221, take Rte. 654 west to Rte. 653 north to Rte. 660 west.
	Howells Creek	
	Laurel Fork	From Laurel Fork on Rte. 58, take Rte. 638 north to Rte. 630 west.
	Little Indian Creek	From Rte. 221, take Rte. 622 north to Rte. 612 north to Rte. 751 east.

	Little River	
	Mira Fork	From Rte. 621, take Rte. 623 north to Rte. 756 north to Rte. 760 east.
	Rush Fork	
	West Fork Little River	
Fluvanna	Hardware River	
Franklin	Pigg River	
	Runnett Bag Creek	From Blue Ridge Pkwy., take Rte. 793 south to Rte. 792 south.
Frederick	Clearbrook Lake	In the town of Clearbrook.
	Hogue Creek	
	Paddy Run	From Star Tannery, take Rte. 604 west to Rte. 600 south to Rte. 601 west.
	Winchester Lake	
Giles	Big Stoney Creek	From Columbia Furnace on Rte. 42, take Rte. 648 or 675 south.
	Dismal Creek	From Crandon, take Rte. 42 east to Rte. 606 north. Follow signs to Dismal Falls.
Grayson	Big Wilson Creek	From Volney, take Rte. 58 west to Rte. 717 north.
	Elk Creek	From Rte. 21, take Rte. 658 west to Rte. 663 south to Rte. 662 west.
	Fox Creek	From Troutdale on Rte. 16, take Rte. 603 west.
	Hales Lake	
	Helton Creek	From Volney, take Rte. 58 west to Rte. 783 north.
	Middle Fox Creek	
Greene	South River	
	Swift Run	From Standardville, take Rte. 230 north to Rte. 621 north.
Henry	Smith River (Dam)	
	Smith River (Lower)	From Collinsville, take Rte. 57 north.
Highland	Bullpasture River	From McDowell on Rte. 250, take Rte. 654 north or Rte. 678 south.
	S. Branch Potomac River	
Lee	Martins Creek	From Rose Hill on Bus. Rte. 58, take Rte. 672 south to Rte. 682 south.
	North Fork Powell River	From Pennington Gap on Alt. Rte. 58, take Rte. 421 south.
Madison	Hughes River	From Peola Mills on Rte. 231, take Rte. 771 north or south.
	Robinson River	From Banco on Rte. 231, take 670 north.
	Rose River	Continue on Rte. 670 from Robinson.
Montgomery	Craig Creek	From Newport, take Rte. 460 east to Rte. 621 east.

	Pandapas Pond	From Newport, take Rte. 460 to the lake road, which heads west.
	Poverty Creek	From Newport, take Rte. 460 east to Rte. 708 west.
	Toms Creek	From Newport, take Rte. 460 east to Tom's Creek Road north.
Nelson	South Rockfish River	From Greenfield, take Rte. 151 south to Rte. 6 east.
	Tye River	
Page	Cub Run	From Newport on Rte. 340, take Rte. 685 west to FR 65 south.
	Hawksbill Creek	
	Upper Passage Creek	
Patrick	Ararat River	From Mount Airy, take Rte. 104 north. A number of roads to the west and north of 104 cross the river.
	Clarks Creek	
	Dan River	
	Poorhouse Creek	From Stuart on Rte. 58, take Poorhouse Creek Road.
	Rockcastle Creek	From Woolwine, take Rte. 8 north.
	Round Meadow Creek	This creek crosses the Blue Ridge Pkwy. a bit south of Rte. 58.
	South Mayo River (N. Fork)	This river runs along Rte. 58 north of Stuart.
	South Mayo River (South Fork)	
Prince William	Quantico MCB	
Pulaski	Peak Creek	This creek runs through the town of Pulaski.
Roanoke	Glade Creek	This creek runs through the eastern portion of Roanoke and along Webster Colonial Rd. north of the city.
	Roanoke River (City)	The Roanoke runs right through the city.
	Roanoke River Green Hill Park	
	Roanoke River (Salem)	
	Tinker Creek	Tinker runs through the northern part of Roanoke and empties into the Roanoke River.
Rockbridge	Irish Creek	From Irish Gap on the Blue Ridge Pkwy., take Rte. 605 north to Rte. 603 north.
	Maury River	From Cedar Grove on Rte. 39, take Rte. 732 north.
	Mill Creek	From Lexington, take Rte. 11 north to Rte. 645 (Valley Pike) north.
	South River	From Buena Vista, take Rte. 704 north to

		Rte. 631 north to Rte. 608. This road follows the South River in both directions.
Rockingham	Briery Branch Lake	From Briery Branch on Rte. 257, take Rte. 731 south to Rte. 924 west.
	Dry River	
	German River	
	Hone Quarry Lake	From Briery Branch, take Rte. 731 south to Rte. 924 west to Hone Quarry Rd. west.
	Hone Quarry Run	Same as above.
	North Fork Shenandoah	Many accesses to N. F. Shenandoah. Rte. 259 west of Broadway runs along the river.
	Silver Lake	
	Slate Lick Lake	
	Slate Lick Run	
	South River (Grottoes)	From Grottos, take Rte. 340 south. Some of the crossroads to the west cross the river.
Russell	Big Cedar Creek	From Lebanon, Bus. Rte. 19 crosses this creek.
Scott	Bark Camp Lake	Take Alt. Rte. 58 north toward Tacoma from Dungannon, turn on Rte. 706 to Rte. 822, then take Rte. (FR) 993 to the lake.
	Big Stony Creek	From the junction of Routes 23 and 58, take Rte. 871 east to Rte. 653 north to Rte. 619 south.
	Little Stony Creek	
	Stock Creek	
	Straight Fork (Lower)	Follow directions to Big Stony Creek but turn north on Rte. 619, then FR 619.
Shenandoah	Mill Creek	From Hudson Crossroads, take Rte. 42 south. At the junction with Rte. 263, turn west, then south on 612 (Mill Creek Rd.).
	Passage Creek	From the town of Passage Creek, Rte. 678 in both directions follows the river.
	Peters Mill Creek	From Kings Crossing, take Rte. 678 north to Woodstock Tower Rd. west, then south on FR 1702.
	Stony Creek	
	Tomahawk Pond	
Smyth	Comers Creek	From Sugar Grove, take Rte. 16 south to Rte. 650 west.
	Cressy Creek	
	Dickey Creek	From Sugar Grove, Rte. 16 south follows Dickey.
	Hurricane Creek	Follow directions for Comers but turn west off Rte. 650 onto FR 84.

	Middle Fork Holston River (Marion)	The middle fork runs through Marion and parallels I–81 for quite a distance.
	Middle Fork Holston River (Upper)	Same as above.
	South Fork Holston River (Buller Dam)	From Marion, take I–81 west to Adwolf Rd. south, which ends at a tee with Riverside Rd. (Rte. 660). This follows the south fork for quite a distance.
	South Fork Holston River (Lower)	Same as above.
	Staley Creek	From Marion, take Rte. 16 east to Rte. 671 south to FR 243.
Staunton City	Lake Tams	
Tazewell	Lake Witten	
	Laurel Creek	From North Gap, follow Rte. 613 west.
	Lincolnshire Lake	
	Little Tumbling Creek	
Warren	Happy Creek	
Washington	Beartree Lake	
	Big Brumley Creek	From Hayters Gap, take Rte. 689 to the trailhead. This will take some hiking.
	Big Tumbling Creek	From Saltville, take Allision Gap Rd. north to Rte. 613 west to Rte. 747 north.
	Straight Branch	Take Rte. 58 east from its junction with Rte. 91. The river runs along the road. There's a trail upstream.
	Tennessee Laurel	Follow directions to Valley Creek (see below) through Taylor's Valley to Rte. 725. It follows the river in both directions.
	Valley Creek	From Rte. 58 near Green Cove, take Rte. 726 west.
	Whitetop Laurel	From Damascus, take Rte. 58 east. This road follows the river. Where the river swings away from the road, the Virginia Creeper Trail follows the stream. Follow signs to the trail.
Wise	Clear Creek	Clear Creek runs through the town of Ramsey on Rte 74.
	Middle Fork Powell River	From near Norton, take Rte. 610 north. It runs along the river.
	Pound River	Routes 631 and 754 parallel the river above Flannagan around the town of Flemington. Bus. Rte. 23 follows the river near the village of Pound.

	North Fork Pound River	Same as above.
Wythe	Cripple Creek	Rte. 94
	Gullion Fork Ponds	
	Rural Retreat Lake	
	Stoney Creek	
	West Fork Reed Creek	From the crossroads of I–81 and 90, take Rte. 680 north to Rte. 625 north.

Delayed Harvest Trout Streams

This program provides an enhanced trout-fishing experience for anglers. Legal-size fish are stocked in the fall, winter, and spring. From October 1 through May 31, these waters are catch-and-release. In addition, only artificial lures are allowed. From June 1 through September 30, trout may be kept and the general regulations apply. A trout license is required to fish these waters from October 1 through June 15.

90 Accotink Creek (Fairfax County)

The area from Route 236 (Little River Turnpike) to Route 620 (Braddock Road) is a Delayed Harvest area. The best access is in the Fairfax County Park Authority's Wakefield Park facility off Braddock Road.

91 Back Creek (Bath County)

To get to this mountainous stream, take Route 600 north from Mountain Grove for about 6 miles. Back Creek is excellent for fly-fishing and has a moderate gradient. The area has a nice campground and two lakes for fishing bass and other warm-water species.

92 Chestnut Creek (Carroll County)

The Chestnut Creek special-regulations section extends 11.4 miles from the Route 58 Bridge in Galax downstream to its confluence with the New River. The New River Trail parallels the creek. It is a great place to take a backpacking/fishing trip. The trailhead is in Galax, and parking can be found along the roads.

93 Hardware River (Fluvanna County)

Hardware River Wildlife Management Area is the location of this 2.6-mile Delayed Harvest Area. It is very picturesque and extends from Muleshoe Bend downstream. From Scottsville, take Route 6 east, then go south on Route 611 to the Kidd's Mill Road parking area.

94 Holliday Creek (Appomattox/Buckingham Counties)

This creek provides a quality fishing experience for many. It is located in the Appomattox/Buckingham State Forest, starts at Holliday Lake, and runs for 2.8 miles to Route 640. To get here, take Route 24 east out of Appomattox to Route 626 south. Turn east onto 640 and follow to the creek.

95 Holmes Run (Fairfax County)

This urban stream flows out of Lake Barcroft for 1.2 miles. It boasts some excellent fishing. Access the trail following the stream off Route 244 (Columbia Pike).

96 North Fork of Pound River and Pound River (Wise County)

This 2-mile stretch starts at the confluence of Indian Creek and runs upstream to the dam on the North Fork. Anglers can get to the river at the North Fork Dam and from the town of Pound.

97 North River (Augusta County)

Foot trails lead to this area. It extends from Elkhorn Dam downstream 1.5 miles to the top of the Staunton City Reservoir. Anglers can park at Elkhorn Lake and hike.

98 Passage Creek (Warren County)

From the Warren County line downstream, this area runs approximately 1 mile. Park off Route 678 or 619 to access the area.

99 Peak Creek (Pulaski County)

This area extends from Tract Fork downstream to the Route 99 bridge for about 2.7 miles. It runs through downtown Pulaski.

100 Pedlar River (Amherst County)

From Lynchburg City Reservoir, southeast of Buena Vista, this area extends for 2.7 miles. Three access points to the river are located along FR 39 off Route 607. Be prepared to hike.

101 Roanoke River (Roanoke County and City of Salem)

Near Roanoke, two Delayed Harvest areas are available to anglers. One is in Green Hill Park off Route 11/460 and the other is in the city of Salem. The Green Hill Park section runs for about a mile. It is best accessed from the park. The Salem section runs along Riverside Drive and can be accessed from this road.

102 South River (Augusta County)

In Waynesboro a Delayed Harvest area extends from the 2nd Street Bridge upstream 2.4 miles to Rife Loth Dam.

Fee Trout-fishing Areas

Depending on location, the fee fishing areas are available intermittently from the first Saturday in April to the end of September. These waters are stocked a few times every week throughout the season. This makes for a quality fishing experience. In addition to a Virginia Freshwater Fishing license, a daily permit is required during the fee fishing season in these waters. When the areas are not open for fee fishing, they revert to designated stocked trout waters and a trout license is required. Check the legal creel and size limit with the Virginia Department of Game and Inland Fisheries (VDGIF).

103 Clinch Mountain Fee Fishing Area

Fee fishing in this area is operated from the first Saturday in April through September. It is located about 7 miles west of Saltville. The area consists of approximately 7 miles of relatively fast water. This is real mountain trout fishing because Big Tumbling Creek has a very steep gradient stream with numerous small waterfalls and large, deep rocky pools. Stockings take place Monday through Saturday. Fishing begins at 6:00 A.M. daily, except on opening day. Camping is available at the area and the Virginia Department of Game and Inland Fisheries (VDGIF) owns and manages the surrounding land. From Saltville, take Allision Gap Road north to Route 613. Go west to Route 747 and take it south.

104 Crooked Creek Fee Fishing Area

Fee fishing in this area is operated from the first Saturday in April through September. The creek is located about 5 miles east of Galax in Carroll County. Five miles of stream is stocked Monday through Saturday. A portion of this stream is designated as a Wild Trout Fishery. Crooked Creek is slower than Big Tumbling Creek. The land along the banks is a mix of woods and fields. No camping facilities are available at Crooked Creek. To get there from Galax take Route 58/221 east. Before crossing Crooked Creek take Route 722 south to Route 713. Take Route 713 east, then take Route 712 south.

105 Douthat Lake Fee Fishing Area

The Douthat Lake Fee Fishing Area is located within the state park that bears its name. It is open from the first Saturday in April through June 15 and then again from September 15 through October 31. The area includes the 60-acre Douthat Lake and about 4 miles of Wilson Creek.

During the summer, no stockings take place and no fee is required. This is a great place to introduce a kid to fishing. A "children only" area is available. Kids under twelve can fish without a permit as long as they are accompanied by an adult. However, the combined total take can not exceed that of the adult.

The Fingerling Stocking Program

This program stocks small trout into cold-water streams and lakes, that is, waters that remain viable for trout year-round. This adds opportunities for anglers to catch trout that have adapted to the wild, therefore enhancing the trout-fishing experience.

Additional regulations have been applied to certain waters in this program. Some are fly-fish only, others single hook, many catch-and-release, and others have larger size and smaller bag limits. Restrictions have been applied to certain Wild Trout Waters as well as several types of stocked trout streams to provide anglers with the opportunity to catch more and larger trout throughout the fishing season. These special-regulations areas include some of the state's best trout waters and are described in detail in this guide.

Trophy Trout Water

Below find a list of waters that are stocked with fingerlings. These lakes and streams can support trout year-round. This enables the fish to grow large. Most have special regulations, so be sure to check with the Virginia Department of Game and Inland Fisheries (VDGIF) before casting your lines.

Trout Lakes

Due to Virginia's warm climate, only a few lakes can support trout year-round. These are either located at high elevations or are deep enough to become stratified during the summer. One site, Lake Moomaw in Alleghany/Bath Counties, is covered elsewhere in this book (Site 72). Other lakes are as follows:

106 Laurel Bed Lake (Russell County)

This lake is located in the Clinch Mountain Wildlife Management Area and covers about 330 acres. It is stocked with small brook trout each fall and they appear to do quite well. Most fish with worms, mealworms, or flies. The best angling is in June.

From Route 19, head south on Route 642, then follow the unimproved road or trail to the south. You can also take Allison Gap Road north from Saltville, then head east on Route 613 to Route 667 north. Then follow the trail (unimproved road).

107 Lexington City Reservoir (Rockbridge County)

This high-elevation lake is a put-and-grow water. It covers 22 acres and is stocked with brookies. Many measure between 9 and 13 inches. Check to see if a special license from the city is required.

From Lexington, take Route 11 south to Route 251 south. Then take Route 677 west to Route 612, which might require foot travel.

For more information, contact Lexington City Hall at (540) 462-3702.

108 Mills Creek and Coles Run Reservoirs (Augusta County)

These ponds are stocked with fingerling brook that grow to 12 inches.

From Buena Vista, take Route 60 east to the Blue Ridge Parkway north. Turn north onto FR 162 to the trailhead. It is a good hike.

109 Skidmore Lake (Switzer Dam, Rockingham County)

This 104-acre impoundment grows brookies to 2 or 3 pounds. It also supports a warm-water fishery.

From Rawley Springs, take Route 33 north to FR 227 south.

Trout Rivers

Some trout rivers have been covered elsewhere in this book. These are the Jackson River in Alleghany County (Site 71) and the Pound River in Dickenson County (Site 75). Others are as follows:

110 Smith Creek (Alleghany County)

Small browns are stocked from the Forest Service boundary upstream about 2.5 miles to the Clifton Forge Dam. Many 8-to-2-inch fish are taken with some up to 20 inches reported.

From Clifton Forge, take Route 606 northwest. Park at the entrance to the Clifton Forge Water Plant and walk a half mile to the river.

111 Snake Creek (Carroll County)

This stream yields browns up to 4 pounds. It is located below the junction of Routes 922 and 674 just north of Fancy Gap.

Trophy Trout

The streams below are high quality and considered trophy trout waters. Check with the Virginia Department of Game and Inland Fisheries (VDGIF) in advance for current regulations.

112 Buffalo Creek (Rockbridge County)

The area runs for 2.9 miles from Colliers Creek to the confluence of the North and South Forks of Buffalo Creek. Browns and rainbows are stocked and plenty of 10-to-16-inch fish are caught. Some 5-to-8-pounders have been taken.

From Lexington, take Route 251 south.

113 The Dan River (Patrick County)

This 6-mile segment of stream extends from Talbott Dam downstream to the Townes Reservoir. Trout reproduce naturally here, and plenty of 8-to-12-inch fish are caught.

Take Route 614 south from Meadows of Dan to Route 601 south.

For more information, contact the City of Danville, Director of Electric Division, Department of Utilities, P.O. Box 3300, Danville, VA 24543; (434) 799–5270.

114 Roaring Run (Botetourt County)

This 1-mile section of stream is located in the Jefferson National Forest downstream of the Botetourt County line. Small browns and rainbows are stocked, and fish up to 16 inches are caught. Take Route 621 north from Strom to get here.

115 Smith River (Henry County)

This area starts at Route 666 in the town of Bassett and runs upstream to Town Creek about 2½ miles before Philpott Dam. The best way to access the area is to park at either end and walk.

Call the Army Corps of Engineers (276) 629–2432 to check the water level before you go fishing.

The Wild Trout Program

This program is designed to help wild-trout populations. Virginia is rather warm in the summer, which, along with diminished water flow, works to decrease the amount of trout habitat. The reduction in stream velocity also results in additional siltation, reduction of good fish cover, and channel alteration. These all make life for trout more difficult.

The maximum temperature of many of Virginia's shaded mountain streams does not exceed 70 degrees F during the hottest part of the summer. This is within the tolerable range for trout.

Habitat alteration by humans has also cost Virginia many miles of trout water. For example, trout need undercut banks and vegetation overhangs to hide in. In addition, forage is reduced by siltation because of the decreased insect populations.

These are just a few of the factors that affect a cold-water fishery. In the past, Virginia lost many good wild trout populations due to habitat degradation caused by widespread channelization, logging techniques, removal of streamside vegetation, intensive agriculture, and other causes.

The Wild Trout Program was started to stop this loss of habitat and to aid in the restoration of that which is already lost. Since these cold-water fish have a much harder time reproducing than their warm-water kin, additional regulations had to be applied. It is apparently succeeding. With over 2,300 miles of wild streams supporting the state's only native trout, brookies, biologists are optimistic. Growth for this species in Virginia is much faster than that in any other state. This means that the habitat is healthy.

Wild Trout Streams

Some of the wild trout streams have been covered elsewhere in this book. These are the St. Mary's River in Augusta County (Site 73), the South Fork of the Holston River in Smyth County (Site 86), and Whitetop Laurel Creek in Washington County (Site 89). Other wild trout streams are as follows:

116 North Fork Moormans River (Albemarle County)

Fishing in the upper areas of this river is still good. Be prepared to hike. Take Route 250 west of out of Charlottesville to Route 680 north. Follow this to White Hall, then go west onto Route 614, which follows the Moormans River to Sugar Hollow

Reservoir. This is also known as the Charlottesville Reservoir. After passing the lake, you'll see a trailhead. Park here and hike up the north fork. Walk as far as you wish. It seems the farther up the better the fishing.

117 Buffalo River (Amherst County)

Eight-to-ten-inch brookies will be found in the upper region of this stream. It is relatively fast, with boulders and nice pools.

In Amherst turn west onto Route 60 and follow it to the forks of the Buffalo. Head north on Route 635, follow it to the end, and hike.

118 Ramsey's Draft (Augusta County)

Ten miles of native brook trout water is found along this stream, with the best fishing available in the spring.

Take Route 250 west from Staunton and pass through Churchville. At the mountain home picnic area sign, turn right and hike up the trail.

119 North Creek (Botetourt County)

Wild rainbows as well as brookies inhabit the upper reaches of this stream. From the North Creek campground, fish upstream. Twelve-inch trout are caught here.

Take Route 11 north from Buchanan to Route 614 (Arcadia Road) east. Take FR 21 east to Arcadia, then North Creek Road (FR 59) east past the campground.

120 North and South Forks of Stewart's Creek (Carroll County)

This native brook trout stream in the Stewart's Creek Wildlife Management Area has numerous pools, good cover, and a high gradient. To get here from Galax, take Route 97 southeast to southwest on the Blue Ridge Parkway. Follow the signs to Stewart Creek WMA.

121 Little Stony Creek (Giles County)

The upper reaches of Little Stony Creek is home to brook and rainbow trout. Downstream, rainbows predominate. Seven-to-twelve-inch fish are common. The area is heavily used by hikers and picnickers.

To get here, take Route 623 north from Penbroke.

122 East Fork of Chestnut Creek (Carroll County)

Brookies up to 13 inches or more are caught here. Don't get confused: It is also known as Farmer's Creek. Lower areas are slower than the upper waters.

Take Route 89 south out of Galax to the Blue Ridge Parkway north. The east fork crosses the Blue Ridge near the line between the two counties. Fish upstream.

123 Big and Little Wilson Creeks and Their Tributaries (Grayson County)

Wild rainbows and native brook trout are caught out of these streams. Brookies are more common in the upper reaches while rainbows are found throughout the streams. This place is really pretty with great-looking pools. Hiking is best.

To get here, head north on Route 58 from Mouth of Wilson. At Volney, Route 58 follows the Big Wilson. To get to the Little Wilson, take Route 16 north to Route 738 west. Access to the upper reaches of the Big Wilson is through Grayson Highlands State Park on Route 817 off Route 58.

124 Conway River/Devils Ditch (Greene County)

These streams run through the Shenandoah National Park and the Rapidan Wildlife Management Area. Seven-to-eleven-inch brookies are common in the upper reaches and browns to 20 inches in the lower portions.

From Graves Mill, take Route 615 west to Route 426 west.

125 Rapidan River (Madison County)

Good numbers of 10-to-12-inch brookies are caught here, in Virginia's most popular trout stream.

Route 662 both north and south from Graves Mill runs along the river. To get to the upper reaches, take Route 649 from Criglersville.

126 Little Stony Creek (Shenandoah County)

Brookies from 7 to 10 inches are found in this small stream. To get here from Columbia Furnace, take Route 675 west to Route 749 north.

This just a sampling of Virginia's wild trout waters. The Shenandoah National Park has many more. Special regulations apply to most wild trout streams. To preserve the resource, become familiar with them.

Trout Heritage Day Program

While trout fishing is now available year-round, it was not always so. In the past the first Saturday in April marked opening day for trout fishing. For nostalgic reasons, a program was added several years ago for those anglers who enjoyed and missed the old opening day. Certain streams are now stocked for the first Saturday in April. Those waters are closed a few days before the event to simulate historic conditions. We do not list any here because they change frequently. See the Department of Game and Inland Fisheries (VDGIF) Web site for information (www.dgif .virginia.gov/fishing/).

This section lists a number of urban fishing locations. We give the species available and directions. Some of these waters have been described in detail in other chapters of this book and covered on other maps. See below for such references.

Many of these lakes and streams are fine for a simple day outing for a family, perhaps in combination with other activities like a picnic. Other waters support good piscatorial populations and provide some fantastic sport.

Charlottesville

127 Ragged Mountain Reservoirs

These two small lakes are part of the city's water supply. Boats are allowed but must be carried to the lakes, and parking here is limited. The reservoirs are open from sunrise to sunset. The key species here are largemouth bass and bluegill. To get here, take Route 29 south to Route 702 west.

128 Rivanna Reservoir

This 450-acre lake a short distance from Charlottesville offers fishing for largemouth bass, bluegill, and redear sunfish. It's open from sunrise to sunset, and gasoline engines are not permitted. To get here, take Route 29 north to Route 631 west to Route 659 north or 676 north.

D.C. Metropolitan Area in Virginia

Some sites near the D.C. area have been covered elsewhere in this book. See Riverbend Park (site 24), Burke Lake (site 27), and Accotink Lake in the Fairfax County section of the Catchable-trout Stocking Program chart.

129 Algonkian Regional Park

This Potomac River park has good fishing and is a great place to take kids. The key species here are large- and smallmouth bass, bluegill, catfish, crappie, and carp. To get here from the Capital Beltway (Interstate 495), take Route 7 west to Cascades Parkway north to the park.

130 Cameron Run Regional Park (Lake Cook) (see map on page 55)

Lake Cook is a perfect place to have a picnic and take kids fishing. The park has many other activities for those who do not wish to fish. The key species are trout in winter, bluegills, largemouth bass, crappie, and perch. Shore fishing only.

To get here, in Alexandria take exit 174 from the Capital Beltway, turn north onto Eisenhower Avenue, and follow it to the park on the west side of the road.

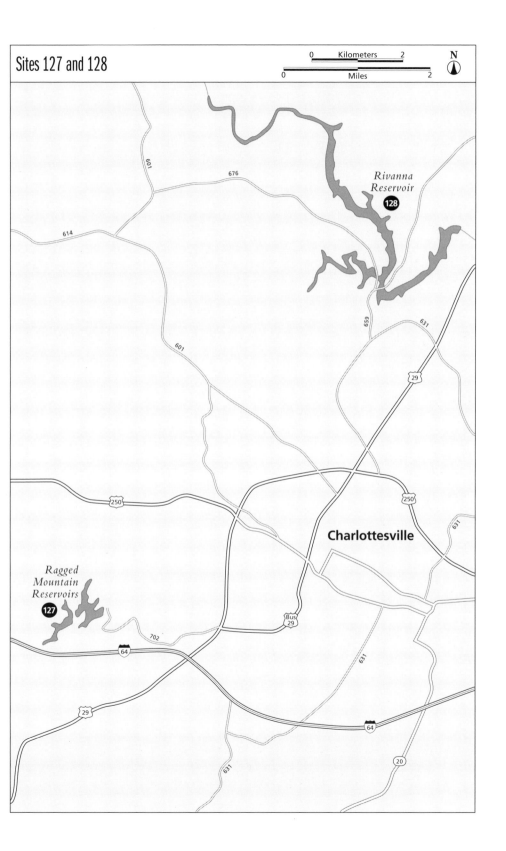

Sites 127 and 128

131 Fountainhead Regional Park *(see map on page 55)*

Located on Occoquan Reservoir, the key species to be found at this park are large-mouth bass, crappie, channel and flathead catfish, and bluegill. To get here from Interstate 95 in Woodbridge, take Route 123 north to Route 647 west and follow the signs to the park.

For more information, contact the park at 10875 Hampton Rd., Fairfax Station, VA; (703) 250–9124; www.nvrpa.org/fountainhead.html.

132 Mason Neck State Park *(see map on page 55)*

This park offers fresh- and brackish-water fishing a short distance south of the D.C. area. The key species to be found here are bass, striped bass, perch, catfish, eels, sunfish, and carp. The park is about 20 miles south of D.C. Take Route 1 south, then proceed east on Route 242 (Gunston Road) to the park entrance.

For more information, contact Mason Neck State Park at 7301 High Point Rd., Lorton, VA 22079-4010; (703) 339–2385 or (703) 339–2380; www.dcr.state.va.us/parks/masonnec.htm.

Richmond

133 Bryan Park

A great place to bring kids, the key species at this park are sunfish, catfish, and a few bass. Get here via Bellevue Avenue and Hermitage Road. To get there, take Interstate 64 to Route 33 and go north. Turn east on Dumbarton Road, then south Stoneleigh Road. Turn east on Bryan Park Road to the lake.

134 Byrd Park

Three fishing lakes are offered at Byrd Park. The key species to be found here are largemouth bass, bluegill, sunfish, and channel catfish. The lakes are stocked regularly and provide excellent family fishing. To get there from Interstate 64 take North Boulevard (Route 161) south. Turn east on Idlewood, then south on South Davis. This takes you to one of the lakes. Another is found by continuing south on South Davis and then heading east on Lakeview to the lake. The third lake can be accessed by foot from there. Follow the path.

135 Dorey Lake Park

The key species at this five-acre lake are catfish, largemouth bass, bluegill, redear, and an occasional crappie. To get here, from Interstate 64 turn south on Laburnum Avenue then left (east) on Darbytown Road. Follow this road to the park.

136 Great Shiplock Park

River fishing for white perch, shad, herring, rockfish, and catfish is available at this park. It's located at Dock and Pear Streets. To get here, take the East Broad Street exit off Interstate 95 and go east. Turn south on North 25th Street, then east on East

Sites 133, 134, 135, 136, and 137

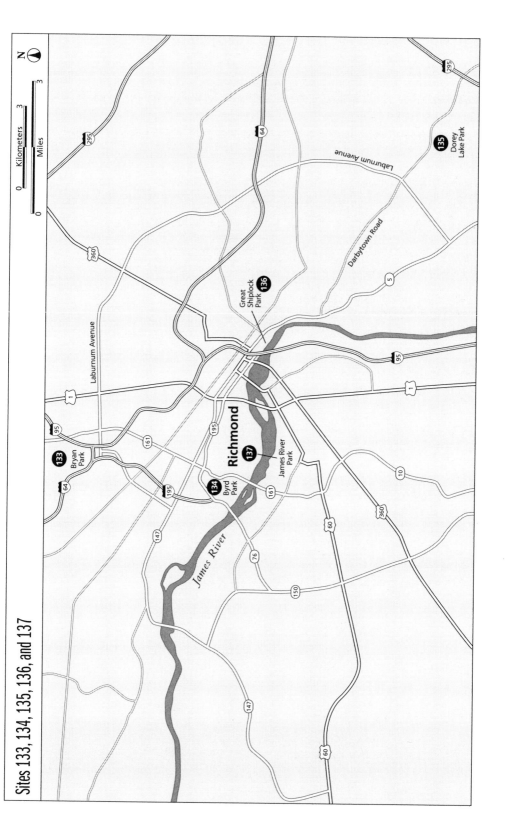

Main Street to south on Pear Street. Follow to the park.

137 James River Park

Richmond's largest park runs along the river and provides excellent fishing for catfish, musky, and small, bigmouth, and spotted bass. The park runs from the Huguenot Bridge in the west to a half mile beyond the Interstate 95 bridge in the east. It includes most of the fall line of the river within Richmond City limits. To get to the largest section of the park, take the Route 147 exit west off Interstate 195. Follow Route 147 across the Huguenot Bridge and turn east on Riverside Drive. Follow Riverside to the park. For more information, visit www.jamesriver.org.

Virginia Beach and Surrounding Areas (Hampton Roads)

Some sites in Hampton Roads have been covered elsewhere in this book. In addition to those detailed below, see First Landing State Park (site 21), False Cape State Park (site 22), and Lakes Whitehurst and Smith (site 50).

138 Bayville Farms Park *(see map on page 45)*

The park offers a small pond that provides fishing for sunfish, cats, and a few small bass. To get there from Interstate 64 take the Route 13 exit north to Route 60. Go east on Route 60, then south on Baylake Road. Follow it to the park.

For more information, contact the park at 4132 First Court Rd., Virginia Beach, VA 23455; (757) 460–7569.

139 Lake Prince

The key species to fish for here are striped bass, largemouths, crappie, bluegill, and catfish. The lake is located in Norfolk, off Route 460 at Providence Church on Route 604 (Lake Prince Road) in Suffolk. Bank fishing is restricted to a small area around the boat ramp.

140 Little Island Park *(see map on page 45)*

This 144-acre beach park provides fishing for both salt- and freshwater fish, plus great crabbing. It's located in the extreme south of Virginia Beach along the coast.

141 Mount Trashmore Park *(see map on page 45)*

The two lakes at this park offer good fishing for largemouth bass, sunfish, white perch, and carp. It's located at South Boulevard and Edwin Drive. Take the South Independence Boulevard exit south off Interstate 264. Turn north on Edwin Drive to one of the lakes. The other lake can be found by continuing north on Edwin and then going east on South Boulevard. Follow that to the lake.

Index

A

Abel Reservoir (Safford County Reservoir) 68
Accotink Creek (Fairfax County) 148
Algonkian Regional Park 156
Appomattox River 101
Arrowhead Lake 64
Assateague Island 16

B

Back Bay 95
Back Creek (Bath County) 148
Bark Camp Lake 132
Bayville Farms Park 160
Bear Creek Lake 99
Beaver Lake 102
Beaverdam Creek Reservoir 53
Briery Creek Lake 104
Brunswick County Lake 107
Bryan Park 158
Buffalo Creek (Rockbridge County) 152
Buffalo River (Amherst County) 154
Buggs Island Lake (Kerr Reservoir) 111
Burke Lake 54
Byrd Park 158

C

Cameron Run Regional Park (Lake Cook) 156
Cape Charles 28
Chandler's Mill Pond 75
Charlottesville 156
Chestnut Creek (Carroll County) 148
Chickahominy River and Lake, Lower 87
Chincoteague 13
Claytor Lake 127

Clinch Mountain Fee Fishing Area 150
Clinch River 133
Colonial Beach 32
Crooked Creek Fee Fishing Area 150

D

D.C. Metropolitan Area in Virginia 156
Dan River (Patrick County) 152
Dan River 109
Diascund Creek Reservoir 81
Dorey Park Lake 158
Douthat Lake Fee Fishing Area 150

E

East Accotink Creek (Fairfax County) 148
Eastern Shore (saltwater fishing) 9
  Atlantic Ocean Side 13
  Chesapeake Bay Side 25

F

False Cape State Park 46
Fee Trout-fishing Areas 149
Fingerling Stocking Program 150
First Landing State Park 46
Flannagan Reservoir 122
Fountainhead Regional Park 158

G

Gardy's Mill Pond 74
Gargatha 18
Gatewood Reservoir 126
Gloucester Point Fishing Pier 37
Great Creek Watershed Lake 108
Great Falls National Park 51
Great Shiplock Park 158
Great Wicomico River (Reedville Area) 32

H

Hampton Roads 160
Hardware River (Fluvanna County) 148
Holliday Creek (Appomattox/Buckingham Counties) 148
Holliday Lake 99
Holmes Run (Fairfax County) 149
Holston River, Middle Fork 137
Holston River, North Fork 135
Holston River, South Fork 136

J

Jackson River 115
James River Bridge 40
James River Park 160
James River, Lower 84
James River, Upper 97

K

Kerr Reservoir 111
Kiptopeke State Park 30

L

Lake Airfield 89
Lake Anna 71
Lake Brittle 58
Lake Chesdin 103
Lake Cook 156
Lake Frederick 54
Lake Gaston 113
Lake Gordon 109
Lake Gordonsville (Bowlers Mill) 70
Lake Moomaw 117
Lake Orange 68
Lake Prince 160
Lake Smith 89
Lake Whitehurst 89
Laurel Bed Lake (Russell County) 151
Leesville Lake 131
Leesylvania State Park 64
Lexington City Reservoir (Rockbridge County) 151

Little Creek Reservoir 83
Little Island Park 160
Little Stony Creek (Giles County) 154

M

Mason Neck State Park 158
Mattaponi River 75
Maury River 119
Meherrin River 106
Mills Creek and Coles Run Reservoirs (Augusta County) 151
Moormans River, North Fork (Albemarle County) 153
Mount Trashmore Lake 160

N

New River 123
North Creek (Botetourt County) 154
North Landing River 93
North River (Augusta County) 149
Northern Virginia (freshwater fishing) 51
Nottoway River 90

O

Occohannock Creek 27
Occoquan Reservoir 57
Occoquan River 56
Ocean View Pier 43
Onancock Creek 26
Oyster 23

P

Pamunkey River 78
Passage Creek (Warren County) 149
Peak Creek (Pulaski County) 149
Pedlar River (Amherst County) 149
Philpott Reservoir 131
Piankatank River 35
Piankatank River/Dragon Run 79
Plum Tree Island National Wildlife Refuge 40
Pocahontas State Park: Swift Creek

Lake and Beaver Lake 102
Pound River 121
Pound River and North Fork Pound
    River (Wise County) 149

Q
Quinby 19

R
Ragged Mountain Reservoirs 156
Ramsey's Draft (Augusta County) 154
Rappahannock River 35
Rappahannock River, Lower 69
Rappahannock River, Upper 66
Reedville Area 32
Richmond 158
Rivanna Reservoir 156
Riverbend Park 52
Roanoke River (Roanoke County and
    City of Salem) 149
Roaring Run (Botetourt County) 152

S
Sandy River Reservoir 105
Saxis 25
Shenandoah River, North Fork 59
Shenandoah River, South Fork 62
Skidmore Lake (Switzer Dam, Rock-
    ingham County) 152
Smith Creek (Alleghany County) 152
Smith Mountain Lake 128
Smith River (Henry County) 153
Snake Creek (Carroll County) 152
South Holston Reservoir 138
South River (Augusta County) 149
South-central Virginia (freshwater
    fishing) 97
Southeastern Virginia (freshwater fish-
    ing) 81
Southwestern Virginia (freshwater
    fishing) 115
St. Marys River 118
Stewart's Creek, North and South

Forks (Carroll County) 154
Swift Creek Lake 102

T
Trout Fishing 141
Trout Heritage Day Program 155

U
Urban Fishing 156

V
Virginia Beach 44
Virginia Beach and Surrounding Areas
    (Hampton Roads) 160

W
Wachapreague 19
Western Branch Reservoir 92
Western Shore 32
Whitetop Laurel Creek 139
Wild Trout Program 153

About the Authors

Ruta Vaskys and Martin Freed have had a number of careers including faculty appointments at various colleges and as entrepreneurs. In the past they earned a living trapping in the winter and collecting wild herbs during the summer in Vermont and Alaska. In addition to the other activities, during the past twenty years they have been outdoors and conservation writers and photographers.

Martin Freed and Ruta Vaskys

Ms. Vaskys has a bachelor of science degree in occupational therapy and a masters in counseling. She has worked in both fields as well as being employed as a professional commercial artist. She studied at the Maryland Institute of Art and the Richmond Professional Institute and did her graduate study at the University of Alaska, Fairbanks.

Mr. Freed taught geology, chemistry, oceanography, and mathematics at a number of colleges and universities. He graduated from Coastal Carolina University with a bachelor of science degree and did his graduate work at the University of Alaska in physical oceanography.

Before going to graduate school, the couple built a cabin in the Green Mountains of Vermont and lived there without electricity or running water for a number of years.

After graduate school, Martin and Ruta made Alaska their home. In 1988 they bought another home on the Eastern Shore of Virginia and currently have residences in Fairbanks and Quinby, Virginia, and split the year between the two.

They started writing outdoors articles in the mid-1980s and have published articles in many regional and national publications, including *Fur, Fish and Game, Easy Street,* the *Eastern Shore News,* the *Mid-Atlantic Fisherman, What's Up Annapolis, Shotgun Magazine,* the *Chesapeake Angler,* the *Salisbury Times, Alaska, Fish Alaska,* and *Fish and Game.* Both are members of the Outdoor Writers Association of America (OWAA).

The couple met on top of Mount Abraham in Vermont in 1976 and have been climbing mountains together ever since.